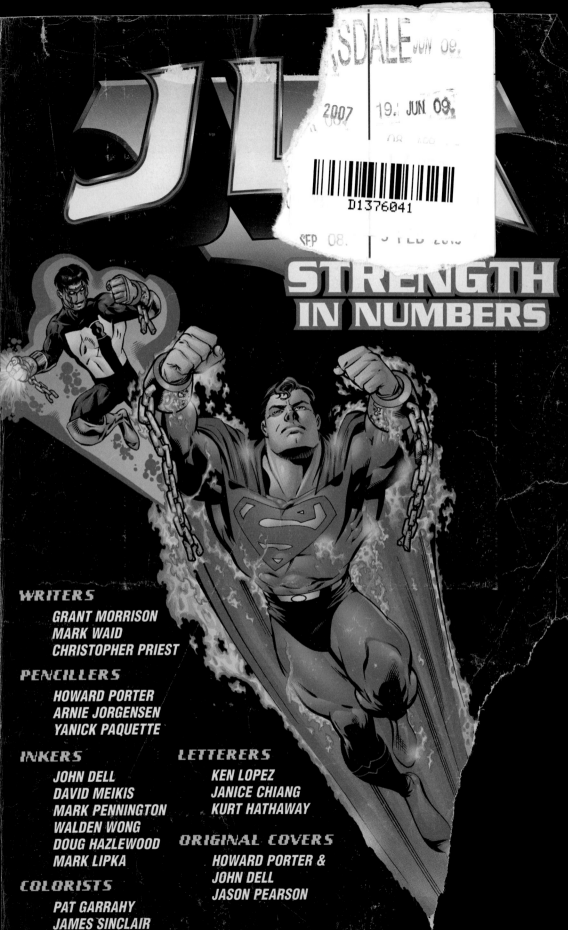

STRENGTH IN NUMBERS

WRITERS

GRANT MORRISON
MARK WAID
CHRISTOPHER PRIEST

PENCILLERS

HOWARD PORTER
ARNIE JORGENSEN
YANICK PAQUETTE

INKERS

JOHN DELL
DAVID MEIKIS
MARK PENNINGTON
WALDEN WONG
DOUG HAZLEWOOD
MARK LIPKA

COLORISTS

PAT GARRAHY
JAMES SINCLAIR

LETTERERS

KEN LOPEZ
JANICE CHIANG
KURT HATHAWAY

ORIGINAL COVERS

HOWARD PORTER &
JOHN DELL
JASON PEARSON

SUPERMAN – The world's greatest super-hero and the guiding force behind this new incarnation of the Justice League. His Kryptonian powers of super-strength, flight and invulnerability temporarily transformed by still-mysterious events, Superman's current energy form is capable of creating a variety of dazzling effects.

BATMAN – Driven by a desire to ensure that others will never experience the tragedy that has shaped his life, Batman uses his keen intellect, a body honed to physical perfection and a vast arsenal of technological and financial resources to wage a personal war against crime on its own shadowy terrain.

WONDER WOMAN – Once Queen of the island nation Themyscira, Hippolyta has assumed the identity of Wonder Woman as penance for her role in the death of her only daughter – Diana, the original Wonder Woman. Possessing augmented strength and stamina, she is a warrior born and has made Diana's crusade for hope and justice her own.

THE FLASH – His name is Wally West – and he is the Fastest Man Alive. The third in a long tradition of super-speedsters, the Flash can tap into an extradimensional "speed force" and reach velocities that approach the speed of light itself.

GREEN LANTERN – One of the youngest members of the team, Green Lantern wields the power ring with which he is able to create solid light images that can be shaped to take any form he can imagine – and imagination is a quality that Kyle Rayner, Green Lantern, has in abundance.

AQUAMAN – Born of an Atlantean queen and an ancient wizard, Aquaman is impervious to the immense pressures of the deep seas, incredibly strong and amazingly fast both in water and on land, and possesses the unique power to telepathically communicate with sea creatures.

J'ONN J'ONZZ, THE MANHUNTER FROM MARS – Pulled across space from his native Mars by Earth science, J'onn J'onzz has been a founding member of every incarnation of the JLA. His many inhuman abilities include the powers of flight, super-strength, telepathy, Martian vision and the natural Martian ability to alter his physical shape and density.

ZAURIEL – A Guardian Angel in Heaven's Eagle Host for over a million years, Zauriel renounced his immortality to serve as Heaven's official champion on Earth. Zauriel's enhanced strength, angel wings, potent sonic cry and supernatural expertise have already proven valuable assets to his teammates.

PLASTIC MAN – While it is easy to believe that Plastic Man was brought into the JLA to be the team's comic relief, this versatile and creative hero was instead chosen for his amazing shapechanging powers and ability to think fast on his feet, and serves with a dedication that often contradicts his easygoing demeanor.

STEEL – Inspired by Superman, the original Man of Steel, John Henry Irons is a man of strong morals and unshakable ethics with the mind of a genius. Armed with his greatest creations – a suit of flight-capable armor and a formidable hi-tech hammer – Steel is the Justice League's resident scientist and techno-artisan.

THE HUNTRESS –Helena Bertinelli is the sole survivor of a brutal attack that killed her parents and closest relations, the Bertinelli crime family. Echoing Batman's own history, Helena became the Huntress and preys on the criminals of the inner city, meting out her own brand of harsh justice.

ORION – Orion of the New Gods lives for one thing, and one thing alone – combat. Son of Darkseid – the evil lord of the planet Apokolips – Orion grudgingly assists the League using his mighty strength and the awesome power of the Astro-Force...all the while waiting to complete his enigmatic mission on Earth.

BIG BARDA – Drilled in the savage art of war by Granny Goodness, Barda as the leader of Darkseid's elite Female Furies battalion the super-escape artist Mister Miracle and joined sent by Highfather, leader of New Genesis, to aid the on the unpredictable Orion.

ORACLE – No stranger to super-heroics, Barbara the streets of Gotham as the masked hero a vicious attack by the Joker left her wheelchair created the identity of Oracle, a mysterious freelanc who specializes in metahuman activities.

HEROES

CHRISTOPHER PRIEST / WRITER
YANICK PAQUETTE / PENCILLER
MARK LIPKA / INKER
KURT HATHAWAY / LETTERER
PAT GARRAHY / COLORIST
DIGITAL CHAMELEON / SEPARATOR
L.A. WILLIAMS / ASSISTANT EDITOR
DAN RASPLER / EDITOR

NEVER THOUGHT TO *GO* THIS FAR *INLAND.*

IT'S REALLY *BEAUTIFUL.*

AND WE ALMOST *LOST* IT.

AND *MAY* LOSE IT *STILL.* THAT'S WHY WE'RE HERE, ARTHUR.

IT'S WHY WE *DISBANDED* THE LEAGUE.

WE MAY BE MANKIND'S *ONLY HOPE.*

YOU REALLY *BELIEVE* THAT, DON'T YOU?

AND YOU *DON'T* --?

HEROES ARE BORN OF *CIRCUMSTANCE.* WE DON'T WAKE UP ONE MORNING AND PIN ON A *CAPE.*

THERE'S A SENSE OF HIGHER PURPOSE.

I BELIEVE WE PLAY A CERTAIN *ROLE* IN THE SCHEME OF THINGS, BUT IT'S ARROGANT TO PRESUME WHAT THAT ROLE *IS.*

SUPERMAN-- MY PEOPLE SUFFERED A *CATACLYSM* A MILLENNIUM AGO--

--AND NOBODY CAME TO *SAVE US.*

WE SURVIVED.

AND THE PEOPLE OF KRYP-TON DID NOT. IT'S ALL A ROLL OF THE DICE, ARTHUR. WE *DO* WHAT WE *DO.*

AS FOR MY BEING ARROGANT--

--I'VE BEEN CALLED WORSE.

IT'S GETTING DARK-- WE'D BETTER GET GOING.

HE'LL BE HERE SOON...

6

Almost 9PM and the storm's not letting up.

Makes crawling around maintenance tubes a lot like sticking a wet fork into a toaster.

Wonder if HE knows that...

WARNING

ELECTRICAL HAZARD

ARE YOU SET YET?

WORKING ON IT.

THE CLOCK IS RUNNING, ORACLE.

I KNOW. I ALSO KNOW--

He's not listening. He's THERE. In THAT place.

--YOU OWN THE CLOCK.

I'VE GOT TO RIP OUT TWO DOZEN CARDS, REROUTE ALL MY JUMPERS--

Staring down the creatures in his head. A one-track mind with no call waiting.

--UPDATE THE DRIVERS AND REWRITE MY OPERATING SYSTEM--

--AND THEN ADD IN SIX HOURS OF RECONFIGURING ALL OF MY DLL FILES AND UTILITIES.

I'VE READ THE MENU, ORACLE. STEP ON IT.

YOU COULD HELP MY MOTIVATION BY TELLING ME WHY YOU WANT ME TO TAP INTO THE MAIN COMPUTER ON THE JLA WATCH-TOWER.

I HAVE MY REASONS.

GREAT.

THIS IS JUST *SWELL.* WHAT IS IT *NOW*--?

WHAT *RULE* HAVE I TRANSGRESSED *THIS TIME*?

HUNTRESS--

--*THAT* GUY IS A *COP.*

HOW DO YOU KNOW THAT?

IT'S MY *JOB* TO KNOW. AND SINCE YOU *INSIST* ON OPERATING IN *MY TOWN*--

--IT'S *YOUR* JOB TO KNOW, TOO.

THAT *CHECKBOOK* IN HIS BACK POCKET-- HOW MANY *DRUG DEALERS* DO YOU KNOW TAKE *CHECKS*?

IT'S A *PRECINCT FLAG,* HUNTRESS--THERE TO HELP TELL THE *GOOD GUYS* FROM THE *BAD GUYS*--

--SOMETHING YOU *REALLY* NEED TO KNOW HOW TO DO.

ARE YOU *QUITE* DONE?

WEEEROOO WEEEE

JONATHAN AND I ARE TURNING IN.

YOU BOYS HELP YOURSELVES TO THE PIE.

IT WAS A REAL HONOR TO MEET YOU, YOUR HIGHNESS!

PLEASE-- BOWING'S REALLY NOT NECESSARY, MR. AND MRS. KENT.

AND "ARTHUR" WILL DO.

YOU FELLAS WATCH OUT FOR THIS PLANET, NOW, Y'HEAR?

WE WILL-- ASSUMING HE EVER GETS HERE.

HE'S HERE.

I THINK SOMETIMES HE FORGETS I CAN SEE IN THE DARKEST OCEAN DEPTHS.

YES, THAT'S IT. I FORGOT.

THAT SOUNDS LIKELY, DOESN'T IT?

HE'S BEEN WAITING IN THE KITCHEN FOR 15 MINUTES.

SORRY TO KEEP YOU WAITING.

SO, DOWN TO BUSINESS. NEITHER NIGHTWING NOR BLACK CANARY WOULD CONSENT TO JOIN THE LEAGUE. MY LIST IS PLASTIC MAN AND ORACLE. SO FAR.

HOME SWEET HOME

FLO

SO FAR?

I'M STILL WORKING ON ONE OTHER.

WHAT ABOUT CAPTAIN MARVEL? OR FIRESTORM?

THE LEAGUE'S STILL TOP-HEAVY IN BRAWN. WE NEED MORE THINKERS.

WHICH BRINGS US TO MY RECOMMEN- DATION.

STEEL?

STEEL.

I'VE SPOKEN TO RAY PALMER. WHILE HE'S STILL THE ATOM, I DON'T THINK HE'S READY JUST YET FOR THE LEAGUE.

WE SHOULD GIVE HIM SOME MORE ROOM WITH THE TITANS--TALK TO HIM AGAIN IN A FEW MONTHS.

I CONSIDERED ELONGATED MAN, BUT WITH RESPECT TO RALPH, I AGREE THAT PLASTIC MAN HAS MORE VERSATILITY.

AND I'M AFRAID RALPH ISN'T THE ONLY GOOD HERO WHO'S GOING TO BE DISAPPOINTED.

AGREED.

WHAT ABOUT DEALING WITH MYSTICAL THREATS? I THINK ZATANNA MIGHT--

I'VE GOT THAT ANGLE COVERED, SUPERMAN. LEAVE THE OCCULT SPECIALIST TO ME.

DONE.

11

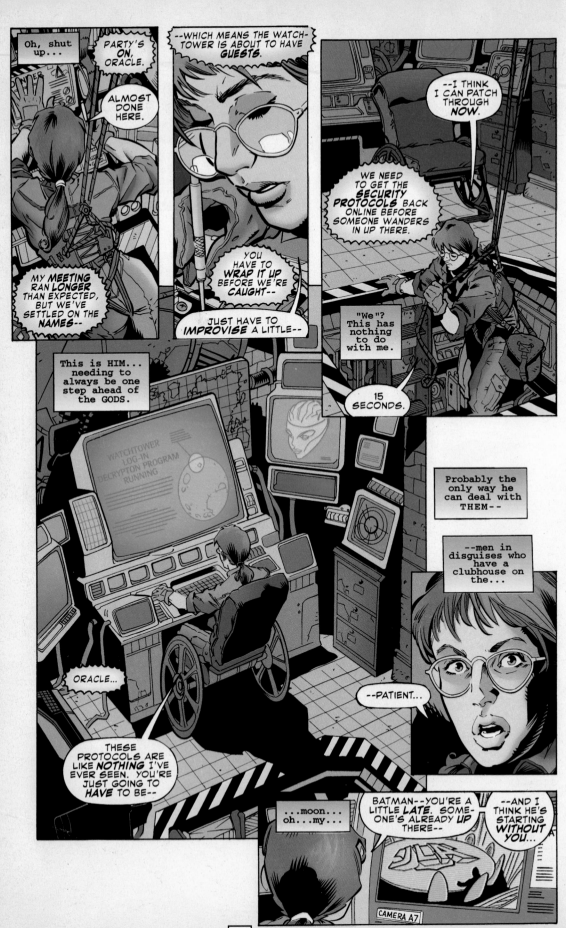

Oh, shut up...

PARTY'S **ON**, ORACLE.

ALMOST DONE HERE.

MY MEETING RAN **LONGER** THAN EXPECTED, BUT WE'VE SETTLED ON THE **NAMES**--

--WHICH MEANS THE WATCH-TOWER IS ABOUT TO HAVE **GUESTS**.

YOU HAVE TO **WRAP IT UP** BEFORE WE'RE **CAUGHT**--

JUST HAVE TO **IMPROVISE** A LITTLE--

--I THINK I CAN PATCH THROUGH **NOW**.

WE NEED TO GET THE **SECURITY PROTOCOLS** BACK ONLINE BEFORE SOMEONE WANDERS IN UP THERE.

"WE"? This has nothing to do with me.

15 SECONDS.

This is HIM... needing to always be one step ahead of the GODS.

WATCHTOWER LOG-IN DECRYPTON PROGRAM RUNNING

ORACLE...

THESE PROTOCOLS ARE LIKE **NOTHING** I'VE EVER SEEN. YOU'RE JUST GOING TO **HAVE TO BE**--

Probably the only way he can deal with THEM--

--men in disguises who have a clubhouse on the...

--PATIENT...

...moon... oh...my...

BATMAN--YOU'RE A LITTLE **LATE**. SOME-ONE'S ALREADY **UP** THERE--

--AND I THINK HE'S STARTING **WITHOUT** YOU...

CAMERA A7

IT'S TRUE. I SWEAR IT...

BLASPHEMER-- ANGELS DON'T SWEAR.

--?! WHO TOLD YOU THAT?

IT IS WRITTEN.

WRITTEN WHERE--?!

IF YOU'RE LOOKING FOR A DATE, I THINK THE ANSWER IS "NO."

--AQUAMAN--?!

I'VE BEEN CALLED THAT.

WHAAAM

UGGHH--!!

SLAM

SO, WHAT GOT THE GOOD SISTER SO RILED UP?

I TOLD HER GOD HAD NO GENDER.

CALLING GOD "HIM" IS A MISNOMER-- IT LIMITS THE PRESENCE TO THE CONFINES OF HUMAN UNDER-STANDING.

AND THEN SHE DECKED YOU.

YES...

...EXCUSE ME... THERE IS EVIL AFOOT.

I DON'T DOUBT IT.

"YOU ARE ONLY FORERUNNERS. PREPARE FOR THE FORTIFICATION OF THE EARTH." THAT'S WHAT *METRON* SAID.

WE'RE *RESTRUCTURING* THE LEAGUE, ZAURIEL. I'D LIKE TO OFFER YOU A SEAT AT THE TABLE.

I'M HONORED.

THE LEAGUE HAS MANY STRENGTHS, BUT WE COULD USE A HERO WITH REAL KNOWLEDGE OF THE SPIRIT WORLD. MAGIC, THE SUPER-NATURAL, THE OCCULT--THAT SORT OF THING.

WELL, IF IT'S *REAL* EXPERIENCE YOU'RE LOOKING FOR, I'M AFRAID I'VE ONLY BEEN DOING THIS SINCE THE DAWN OF TIME.

NOT A PROBLEM. NEVER LET IT BE SAID THAT THE LEAGUE DOESN'T RESPECT THE NEW GUYS.

I'M FLATTERED...BUT DO YOU REALLY BELIEVE HAVING A *FALLEN ANGEL* AMONG YOU WILL BE A *GOOD* THING?

FRIENDS-- OF ANY KIND--ARE A *GOOD THING,* ZAURIEL.

WHAT DO YOU SAY--?

She holds the singular significance--

--of being the one hero in Gotham HE never mentions.

The black sheep of the family.

Makes me wonder what he's UP to--

ROBINSON PARK
Maintenance Shed
#12

--which is something I try NOT to do. Bottom line: Huntress is operating in BATMAN'S town.

And Batman plays for KEEPS.

Making moves only HE understands...

--WHAT-- THE--?!

BATS--AM I EVER GLAD TO SEE--

--Oh.

YOU'RE NOT--I MEAN, I THOUGHT--

--NEVER MIND.

WAIT-- WHO ARE YOU-- AND WHERE--

--WHERE AM I--?

You're in Olympus. Among the Pantheon.

NO TIME-- I'VE GOT TO GET *BACK* IN THERE-- BEFORE THEY *KILL HIM!*

And actually, I think--

--I'd give anything to switch places with you...

GUY...

--YOU'RE BEING AN *IDIOT*, WHICH SHOULD SURPRISE *NO ONE*--!!

LOOK, KID-- *YOU* GUYS *STEPPED OFF*--I SAY *KEEP STEPPING!!*

C'MON, GARDNER--*NO WAY* AM I TAKING *ORDERS* FROM *YOU*--!!

BITE ME, CRAB-FACE--!!

ANYBODY WANTS TO TAKE THE *GAVEL* FROM ME--STEP RIGHT *UP*--!!

FINE.

HAVE IT **YOUR** WAY.

--WAIT 'TIL YOU HEAR MINE.

NOW, UNC-- HOLD IT--THESE GUYS CAME TO THE HOUSE AND DELIVERED A TRANSPORTER TO THE MOON.

I'M SIXTEEN.

FRANKLY-- I THINK THIS IS ON YOUR HEAD.

STEEL--!!

--I DIDN'T EXPECT YOU--I'M PLEASED YOU'VE CHANGED YOUR MIND!

I HAVEN'T, SUPERMAN. I JUST CAME TO COLLECT THESE TWO.

Huh? HEY, UNC-- WAIT--

--THE WORLD'S GREATEST HEROES INVITED YOU TO JOIN--AND YOU'RE TURNING THEM DOWN--?!?

YES. NAT--MY RESPONSIBILITY BEGINS AT HOME-- WITH YOU--

JOHN--I'LL BE FINE.

THESE PEOPLE SAVE THE WORLD.

GO SAVE IT WITH THEM.

ALL RIGHT. WE'LL GIVE IT A SHOT.

ON A TRIAL BASIS. AND, FOR ME, HOME COMES FIRST.

I WOULD EXPECT NO LESS OF YOU, MY FRIEND.

GOT HIM OUT OF THE HOUSE.

IT'S TRUE, BORIS.

I JUST GET BETTER WITH AGE.

PROMETHEVS
UNBOUND

THERE WAS A CROOKED MAN

GRANT MORRISON • WRITER ARNIE JORGENSEN • PENCILLER DAVID MEIKIS • INKER
JANICE CHIANG • LETTERER JAMES SINCLAIR • COLORIST HEROIC AGE • SEPARATOR
PETER TOMASI • ASSOCIATE EDITOR   DAN RASPLER • EDITOR

"I USED TO LOVE IT WHEN THE SOUND OF SIRENS AND THE BULLETS JUST FADED AWAY AND I KNEW WE'D OUTSMARTED THEM AGAIN.

"THEY WANT TO BRING US TO *JUSTICE*, SON," MY DAD USED TO SAY. I THOUGHT JUSTICE WAS A *PLACE*.

SEE THIS?

THIS IS THE *FUTURE*.

"IT'S FUNNY.

"IN ANOTHER WORLD, MY DAD WOULD HAVE BEEN THE *RICHEST* MAN IN AMERICA.

BY THE TIME *YOU'RE* ALL GROWN UP, THERE'S GONNA BE A *COMPUTER* IN EVERYBODY'S HOME, OR TRAILER OR WHEREVER THEY *LIVE*.

MAN, THEY'LL PROBABLY BE ABOUT AS SMALL AS *REFRIGERATORS* BY THEN.

WOW.

"I LOVED THEM. I WAS JUST A *KID*.

"I NEVER WANTED IT TO END...

INTENSE.

THAT'S A COOL ORIGIN STORY.

I DIDN'T SPEND MUCH TIME ON *MINE;* I FIGURED THEY'D ONLY USE, *UH...* A *SOUNDBITE.*

THIS IS A KIND OF A WEIRD *PLACE,* HUH? *FIRST* CALL I GOT SAID I WAS TO MEET THE TV PEOPLE DOWN THE *STREET.*

THEN SOME OTHER GUY FROM *WGBS* TOLD ME TO COME *HERE.*

WELL, YOUR NAME'S *RETRO* AND THIS PLACE IS KIND OF *70'S...*

MAYBE. THAT'S INTERESTING.

I DIDN'T KNOW THERE WAS GONNA BE A *VILLAIN* CONTEST WINNER, TOO... *PRO...*METHEUS, RIGHT?

GUESS YOU WORK OUT, HUH?

I DO, TOO.

IT'S NOT LIKE HAVING *REAL* SUPER POWERS THOUGH, I GUESS...

WHAT DOES "PROMETHEUS" MEAN?

IT'S FROM GREEK MYTHOLOGY. HE STOLE *FIRE* FROM THE GODS.

WHAT ABOUT *YOU?* WHAT'S *YOUR...* "ORIGIN"?

I GOT HIT BY RAYS FROM THE *PAST* AND THEY TURNED ME INTO *RETRO.*

"TODAY'S HERO, YESTERDAY'S ATTITUDE!"

"HERE COMES JUSTICE!"

THAT'S WHAT I WISH *REALLY* HAPPENED. I ALWAYS *WANTED* TO BE A SUPERHERO BUT I JUST DON'T HAVE THAT KINDA *LUCK.*

EXCEPT I WON THIS CONTEST AND NOW I GET TO MEET THE *JUSTICE LEAGUE* ON THE *MOON* AND *PRETEND* TO BE A SUPERHERO.

...WHAT WOULD *YOU* DO IF YOU HAD POWERS LIKE *SUPERMAN?*

I DON'T KNOW... I'D DO GOOD DEEDS AND *HELP* PEOPLE, I GUESS.

ME, TOO. THAT'S KINDA WHAT THE WHOLE *RETRO* THING'S ABOUT. I THINK THAT'S WHY THEY CHOSE *ME* OUT OF ALL THOSE OTHER GUYS WITH CLAWS AND CHAINS AND STUFF.

IT'S GETTING *DARK, huh?*

I THINK THEY WANTED TO WAIT TILL THEY COULD GET SOME PICTURES OF US WITH THE *MOON* IN THE BACKGROUND.

OH, RIGHT.

GUESS I'M KINDA NERVOUS ABOUT THE *TELEPORTER...* I JUST WANNA GET THAT PART *OVER* WITH.

DID YOU MAKE UP ANY MORE OF YOUR ORIGIN STORY? THAT WAS PRETTY COOL.

I DECIDED TO *ANNIHILATE* THE FORCES OF JUSTICE.

MAY AS WELL AIM *HIGH*, HUH? HOW DID YOU GET STARTED ON THAT?

"MOM AND DAD HAD... *SAVED* A LOT OF MONEY.

"AND I HAD *CONTACTS*. CONTRARY TO POPULAR BELIEF, THERE *IS* HONOR AMONG THIEVES; THE UNDERWORLD TAKES CARE OF ITS *OWN*.

"ESPECIALLY IF YOU HAVE ENOUGH DIRT ON THE LOCAL MOB BOSS TO BURY HIM FOR A HUNDRED YEARS.

"IT DIDN'T TAKE LONG TO ESTABLISH A NEW IDENTITY...

"I LEFT HOME AT *16*.

"I HAD A LOT TO LEARN."

"I WANTED TO KNOW *EVERYTHING*.

"I WANTED TO BE THE *BEST*, SO THAT WHEN THE TIME CAME, NO ONE COULD *STOP* ME.

"I WALKED AMONG THE RICH AND THE POWERFUL AND ACQUIRED THEIR SECRETS.

"I FOUGHT ALONGSIDE TERRORIST GUERRILLAS IN MIDDLE EASTERN WAR ZONES, I TRAINED WITH *SILAT* MASTERS IN THE JUNGLES OF MALAYSIA.

"I LEARNED HOW TO MAIM AND KILL IN A DOZEN DIFFERENT LANGUAGES.

"AND THEN I WENT HOME TO TAKE CARE OF SOME *BUSINESS*."

DO YOU KNOW WHAT I'M *FEELING* RIGHT NOW?

"BUT I'M GETTING AHEAD OF MYSELF.

"I'D BEEN HALFHEARTEDLY SEARCHING FOR THE ENTRANCE TO *SHAMBALLA*, A MYTHICAL KINGDOM OF EVIL THAT'S SUPPOSED TO EXTEND BENEATH THE TIBETAN PEAKS INTO *MONGOLIA*.

"TO CUT A LONG STORY SHORT... I *FOUND* IT.

"I LIVED THERE FOR ALMOST A *YEAR* BEFORE, WITHOUT A WORD, THE OLD LAMA SUDDENLY APPEARED IN MY ROOM AND BECKONED FOR ME TO *FOLLOW* HIM.

"AND I DID.

"DOWN TEN THOUSAND STAIRS...

"TO *SHAMBALLA*."

"I THINK IT WAS SOME KIND OF *SPACESHIP.*

"I THINK IT WAS *ALIVE,* ALTHOUGH PARTS OF ITS BODY HAD BEEN *EXCAVATED* SO THAT WE COULD PASS THROUGH.

"HE PROMISED HE WOULD SHOW ME THE *SECRET* OF SHAMBALLA; I WOULD OPEN THE INVISIBLE *DOOR.*

"WITH THE KEY TO THE *VOID.*

"I THINK THE MONKS MUST HAVE BEEN *DESCENDED* IN SOME WAY FROM WHATEVER ARRIVED IN THAT SHIP THOUSANDS OF YEARS BEFORE.

"BUT I CAN'T REALLY SAY I *UNDERSTAND* WHAT HAPPENED.

"AFTERWARDS, THE OTHER MONKS JUST LET ME GO. A NEW *LAMA* WAS IN CHARGE AND HE LOOKED JUST LIKE THE *OLD* ONE.

KLIK!

"THEN I GOT A *BETTER* IDEA."

3 MONTHS LATER:

SO, LIKE I WAS SAYING, I FOUND ONE OF THOSE HORRIBLE LETTERS TEENAGERS WRITE TO THEIR GROWN-UP SELVES.

"DEAR LOIS." IT SAID, "BY NOW YOU'RE PROBABLY MARRIED WITH TWO KIDS TO SOME STUPID GUY AND YOU'VE PROBABLY FORGOTTEN THAT YOU EVER WANTED TO WRITE AND HAVE AN EXCITING LIFE LIKE COLLETTE OR DOROTHY PARKER..."

YOU KNOW WHAT? I WANTED TO WRITE BACK AND TELL THIS GIRL ABOUT MY DAY.

"DEAR LOIS, WRONG, KIDDO! I'VE WON A PULITZER. I'M MARRIED TO CLARK KENT, WHO HAPPENS TO BE SUPERMAN AND ALL THREE OF US HAVE BEEN INVITED TO THE MOON FOR DINNER. HOW FAR OUT OF THE ATMOSPHERE DID DOROTHY PARKER EVER GET?"

FIVE MINUTES, MS. GRANT.

TT. EVEN I DIDN'T NEED THIS MUCH TIME IN MAKEUP, LOIS. HOW DAZZLING CAN YOU GET WITHOUT SURGERY?

ARE YOU SURE YOU DON'T MIND TAKING CLARK'S PLACE, J'ONN?

IS IT OKAY IF I DON'T WATCH THIS? SEEING PEOPLE CHANGE SHAPE ALWAYS MAKES ME FEEL KINDA WEIRD.

YOU CAN TURN AROUND NOW, MISS LANE.

I'M DECENT.

CALL ME LOIS, HUH?

PEOPLE ARE GONNA THINK OUR MARRIAGE IS IN RUINS...

...BUT SHORTLY AFTER THE SHOCK ANNOUNCEMENT THAT THE JUSTICE LEAGUE WAS TO BE *DISBANDED*, THIS *PRESS CONFERENCE* WAS CALLED.

WE HAVE TO RECOGNIZE THE FACT THAT THE ORGANIZATION NEEDS A NEW *STRUCTURE* TO BE ABLE TO MORE EFFICIENTLY DEAL WITH THREATS TO HUMANITY.

THAT'S WHY WE'RE NOW EMBARKING ON AN INTENSE SELECTION AND *RECRUITMENT* PROGRAM...

SINCE THAT STATEMENT, SPECULATION HAS BEEN RUNNING HIGH: WHO'S GOING TO MAKE THE FINAL CUT.

AMANDA TRELLACE
WGBS NEWS   LIVE

JLA PRESS CONFERENCE   LIVE

ONE NEW MEMBER WHO'S A *DEFINITE*, AT LEAST FOR TWENTY-FOUR HOURS, IS RETRO. HE'S THE WINNER OF A NATIONWIDE "*JOIN THE JLA FOR A DAY*" CONTEST.

ALTHOUGH, LIKE MOST OF US, RETRO HAS *NO SUPER POWERS*, HE SHOWED STAR QUALITY WHEN HE MET THE PRESS EARLIER THIS EVENING.

LIVING UP TO HIS CATCH-PHRASE, "*TODAY'S HERO, YESTERDAY'S ATTITUDE*," RETRO CHARMED EVEN HARDENED REPORTERS WITH A DOWN-TO-EARTH OUT-LOOK WE THOUGHT HAD DISAPPEARED WITH THE DINOSAURS.

I GUESS I JUST WANT PEOPLE TO KNOW THAT MY GENERATION AREN'T *ALL*, LIKE, TAKING DRUGS AND KILLING ONE ANOTHER IN DRIVE-BYS...

RETRO   LIVE

RETRO   LIVE

49

I ALWAYS LOOKED UP TO THE JUSTICE LEAGUE. I DIDN'T EVER THINK I'D GET TO LOOK THEM IN THE *EYE*.

I GUESS ALL YOU NEED'S A *DREAM* AND TO BE DUMB ENOUGH TO *BELIEVE* IT.

JLA WATCHTOWER MONITOR WOMB.

S.T.A.R. LABS — LIVE

LOOKS LIKE THE GOOD GUYS ARE BACK.

STAY WITH US LIVE ON WGBS FOR THIS HISTORIC BROADCAST FROM THE JUSTICE LEAGUE'S LUNAR WATCHTOWER.

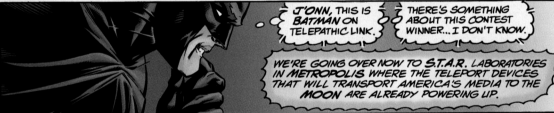

J'ONN, THIS IS *BATMAN* ON TELEPATHIC LINK.

THERE'S SOMETHING ABOUT THIS CONTEST WINNER... I DON'T KNOW.

WE'RE GOING OVER NOW TO *S.T.A.R.* LABORATORIES IN METROPOLIS WHERE THE TELEPORT DEVICES THAT WILL TRANSPORT AMERICA'S MEDIA TO THE *MOON* ARE ALREADY POWERING UP.

ALL HIS MUSCULAR MOVEMENTS AND CHARACTERISTIC *MANNERISMS* ARE AS BEFORE AND SUGGEST A FAIRLY STABLE PERSONALITY TYPE.

HI. THIS IS *LISA HAYMORE* IN THE TELEPORT TUBES HERE AT *S.T.A.R.*

WELL, THEY SAY IT'S LIKE BUNGEE-JUMPING FROM A SUPERSONIC JET AND...

I HOPE THEY'RE LYING.

WGBS NEWS — LIVE

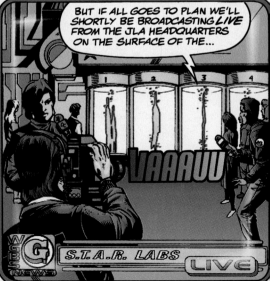

BUT IF ALL GOES TO PLAN WE'LL SHORTLY BE BROADCASTING *LIVE* FROM THE JLA HEADQUARTERS ON THE SURFACE OF THE...

VVAAAUU

S.T.A.R. LABS — LIVE

BOOOM!

HI.

WELCOME TO THE WATCHTOWER.

RETRO. I HOPE WE LIVE UP TO YOUR EXPECTATIONS.

THAT WAS IT? WE'RE HERE?

SUPERMAN?

ONE SMALL STEP.

YOU'RE THE LAST OF THE REPRESENTATIVES FROM THE WORLD'S MEDIA TO ARRIVE, SO IF EVERYBODY WANTS TO FOLLOW ME THROUGH THE RECEPTION GALLERY...

LADIES AND GENTLEMEN...

WONDER WOMAN

PLASTIC MAN

FLASH

AQUAMAN

CAMELOT

GRANT MORRISON—WRITER
HOWARD PORTER— PENCILLER
JOHN DELL— INKER
KEN LOPEZ— LETTERER
PAT GARRAHY— COLORIST
HEROIC AGE— SEPARATIONS
L.A. WILLIAMS— ASS'T EDITOR
DAN RAPLER— EDITOR

...SO, IN ADDITION TO THE PERMANENT CHARTER GROUP OF *SEVEN*, WE'VE ADDED FOUR NEW TEAM MEMBERS AND OUR ROUND TABLE ALSO HAS ONE "FLOATING CHAIR."

THIS WILL BE FOR THE EXCLUSIVE USE OF ANY OF THE *SPECIALIST* SUPERHUMANS WE MAY NEED TO CALL IN AN EMERGENCY SITUATION.

TODAY, IT BELONGS TO *RETRO*.

NOW, MY FRIENDS, IF YOU'LL ACCOMPANY ME THROUGH THE *HALL OF JUSTICE*, WE'LL BEGIN OUR GRAND TOUR IN THE JLA TROPHY ROOM.

SUPERMAN, A GUIDED TOUR IS WELL AND GOOD, BUT I HOPE THERE'LL BE A CHANCE TO ASK YOU ALL A FEW QUESTIONS...

UH... I HAVE A *QUESTION*, PLEASE...

DOES THE MOON HAVE A BATHROOM?

OF COURSE, MS. LANE. THAT'S WHAT THIS CONFERENCE IS ALL ABOUT. IF ANYONE HAS ANY QUESTIONS, PLEASE FEEL FREE TO SPEAK UP.

...YOU'VE TAKEN OVER THE MANTLE OF *WONDER WOMAN* FROM YOUR OWN *DAUGHTER*, AM I RIGHT, *HIPPOLYTA*? AND SHE'S BECOME A GODDESS?

ZAURIEL, YOU'RE AN *ANGEL*, RIGHT?

THIS WAY.

DO YOU HAVE ANY USEFUL ADVICE FOR MENOPAUSAL WOMEN?

SO DOES THAT MEAN THERE REALLY *IS* A GOD?

HA HA HA HA HA HA

HA HA

WHIZ WHIZ

SOMETHING'S WRONG.

I CAN HEAR YOU, BATMAN.

REFRESHMENTS ARE ON THEIR WAY, LADIES AND GENTLEMEN.

I NEED MORE INFORMATION BEFORE I RISK A PANIC HERE.

UH... LISTEN, I... I FEEL A LITTLE QUEASY AFTER THAT TELEPORT RIDE...

WHICH WAY DID STEEL GO?

SECRETS OF THE WATCHTOWER.

HA.

OKAY. ONE DOWN.

AND NOW.

JLA WATCHTOWER Key

EXTERIOR STRUCTURES:
3a Research lab
3b Medical lab
3c Martian Jumpship shuttle hangar
13a Lounge
13b Kitchen
13c Dining area

MAIN VIEW

1 Solar Tower
2 Observation deck
3 Laboratory building
4 Armory
5 Steel's workshop
6 Hall of Justice
7 Monitor Womb
8 Hydroponic forests
9 Aquaman deep water tanks (connected via tunnels to surface pool)
10 Teleporters
11 Reception
12 Secure facility
13 Living quarters
14 Bulk teleport hangar

CROSS-SECTION:

15 Engineering control
16 Trophy room
17 Villain gallery
18 Games/Recreation/Simulators
19 Gymnasium/saunas
20 Pool (connected to deep water tank)
21 Park
22 Private teleporters
23 Air control
24 Tunnels to shuttle bay
25 Stairs to lower levels

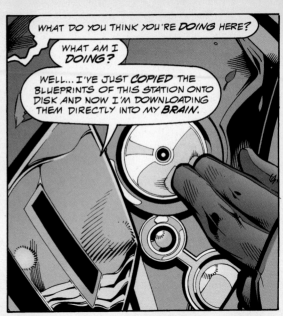

SHWWWUFF

UUUGGHHH

AND *WHILE* YOU'RE *VULNERABLE...*

THIS ONE CONTAINS A MOLECULAR *TOXIN* DESIGNED TO ATTACK YOUR *MORPHOPLASTIC NERVOUS SYSTEM...*

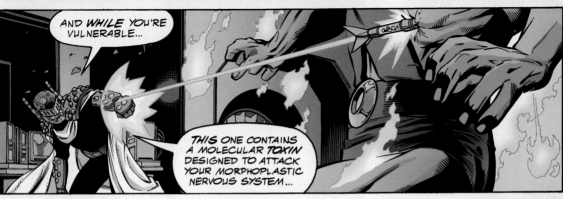

WHAT'S HAPPENING TO MUHHHHH

COMPLETE SPASTIC *PARALYSIS.* YOU NO LONGER HAVE ANY *CONTROL* OVER YOUR *PHYSICAL STRUCTURE.*

IT SHOULD ONLY LAST ABOUT AN HOUR. MUCH LONGER THAN I'M GOING TO *NEED.*

UUUBBBB

UNTIL THEN YOU'RE THE MOST POWERFUL PUDDLE OF GOO ALIVE.

SCOURGE OF THE UNDERWORLD!

HA!

TWO DOWN.

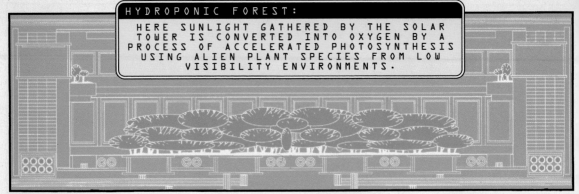

HYDROPONIC FOREST:

HERE SUNLIGHT GATHERED BY THE SOLAR TOWER IS CONVERTED INTO OXYGEN BY A PROCESS OF ACCELERATED PHOTOSYNTHESIS USING ALIEN PLANT SPECIES FROM LOW VISIBILITY ENVIRONMENTS.

IT'S LIKE THE GARDEN OF EDEN.

BUT I GUESS *THAT* WAS FLAMMABLE TOO.

SUPERMAN! WHAT *WAS* THAT?

EVERYBODY STAY CALM.

...THAT'S EASY FOR MISTER INVULNERABLE TO SAY.

IN THE NAME OF THE PRESENCE.

ALERT ALERT ALERT ALERT ALERT ALERT ALERT ALERT ALERT

HEY... AM I *READING* THIS RIGHT?

I HATE TO BE THE ONE TO BRING IT *UP*, BUT... SOMETHING'S HAPPENED TO THE HYDROPONIC GENERATORS, SUPERMAN!

OXYGEN PRODUCTION IS AT *47%* AND FALLING RAPIDLY.

AND...AH...THE SOLAR TOWER'S VENTING *FLAME*.

ALERT ALERT ALERT ALERT ALERT ALERT ALERT ALERT ALERT ALERT ALERT ALERT

I SEE IT.

MY GOD. WHAT'S HAPPENING, SUPERMAN?

DIDN'T YOU *HEAR* THE HAWK GUY? THAT'S OUR *OXYGEN* SUPPLY DISAPPEARING INTO SPACE.

ZAURIEL! HUNTRESS! SECURE THE AREA!

IS THIS SOME KIND OF UNIVERSAL STUDIOS THING AND NOBODY REMEMBERED TO *TELL* ME?

THIS IS FOR THE *CAMERAS*, RIGHT?

SURE. JUST LIKE THE GULF WAR.

ARE WE HAVING OUR FIRST OFFICIAL TEAM-UP, HUNTRESS?

SUPERMAN? HOW SERIOUS IS THIS?

I DON'T KNOW, LOIS. ANY *ONE* OF OUR FOES COULD BE RESPONSIBLE FOR THIS ATTACK.

DON'T WORRY: YOU'RE ALL UNDER THE PROTECTION OF SOME OF THE WORLD'S MOST POWERFUL SUPERHUMANS.

HEY, WHERE DID CLARK GO?

AND I'M TAKING THEM DOWN ONE BY ONE. TEN LITTLE INDIANS.

SCARY, HUH?

STAND AWAY FROM THE EQUIPMENT! LAST WARNING!

WHATEVER THAT *THING* IS, PUT IT *DOWN*.

THIS IS THE *COSMIC KEY*.

PUT IT DOWN OR I *NAIL* YOU TO THE WALL.

WHAT DID YOU DO TO *ZAURIEL*?

IT'S A LONG STORY.

THE KEY OPENS A *DOORWAY* INTO A QUIET LITTLE INFINITY OF *NOTHING*: THE *GHOST ZONE*. I DISCOVERED IT SO I GET TO CALL IT ANY STUPID THING I WANT.

"I HAVE A LITTLE PLACE THERE... I SENT THE ANGEL TO DO SOME FEATHER DUSTING."

GREAT GOD.

HOW DID THAT HAPPEN?

I'M IN LIMBO.

...CONFIRMED: TELEPORT SYSTEMS ARE OFFLINE.

ALSO, I DON'T KNOW IF ANYBODY NOTICED BUT WE LOST OUR TELEPATHIC LINK WHICH MEANS SOMETHING'S HAPPENED TO J'ONN.

HEY, WE'D BETTER CHECK THIS OUT.

WALLY, COME ON. IF THERE ARE BAD GUYS UP HERE, YOU AND ME CAN TAKE THEM OUT IN SECONDS FLAT.

AND AS FOR *YOU*... HAVEN'T YOU BEEN WONDERING WHY I'VE BEEN USING SUCH A LOW, FLAT TONE OF VOICE? WHY MY HELMET LIGHTS HAVE BEEN FLICKERING AT A RATE OF TEN CYCLES PER SECOND?

HYPNOSIS.

YOU CAN'T MOVE UNTIL I SAY SO.

NNN.

SLEEP.

SPANG

ANOTHER COWARD WITH A GRUDGE.

TURN AROUND.

WELL. I'VE BEEN *WAITING* FOR YOU.

I DON'T CARE WHAT YOU'VE BEEN DOING.

IT'S OVER.

SO WE'RE STRANDED HERE WITHOUT *AIR*, IS *THAT* WHAT YOU'RE SAYING, SUPERMAN?

HOW DO WE GET *OFF* OF HERE? I DON'T WANT TO DIE ON THE MOON!

NOBODY'S GOING TO...

LADIES AND GENTLEMEN! HI, THIS IS PROMETHEUS SPEAKING. "TODAY'S ATTITUDE, TOMORROW'S HEADLINES."

HERE'S HOW IT GOES:

I'M HERE TO DESTROY THE JUSTICE LEAGUE. I'M DOING PRETTY WELL, SO FAR. I EXPECT WE'LL BE MEETING SHORTLY SO KEEP THOSE CAMERAS ROLLING!

IT'S A RECORDING.

HIPPOLYTA! GET THESE PEOPLE TO THE *JUMPSHIP* BAY.

I'LL TACKLE THIS "PROMETHEUS."

PROMETHEUS? WHO'S PROMETHEUS?

I THOUGHT I KNEW EVERYONE.

LOOKS LIKE SOMEBODY DESPERATELY WANTS TO BE ON TV, CAT.

AQUAMAN! CAN WE HAVE YOUR COMMENTS?

OUR OXYGEN'S BEING CONSUMED BY FIRE.

I THINK I CAN MANUALLY DIVERT THE CONTENTS OF MY *DEEP WATER* TANKS INTO THE *SPRINKLER* NETWORK.

WE DON'T HAVE TIME FOR COMMENTS.

WROSS

WROSS

WRASP

EVERYBODY, GET TOGETHER.

EVIDENTLY THE WATCHTOWER *IS* UNDER SOME KIND OF ATTACK. I'D LIKE YOU ALL TO FOLLOW ME DOWN TO OUR *SHUTTLE* LAUNCH BAY.

NO ONE WILL DIE. YOU HAVE MY *WORD.*

I HOPE YOUR SHUTTLE'S GOT ROOM FOR A HUNDRED PEOPLE, WONDER WOMAN.

SO WHO'S *PROMETHEUS?*

IS HE ONE OF THOSE DUMB GUYS *YOU* ALWAYS FIGHT?

WHAT? I NEVER *HEARD* OF THE GUY... WALLY, WILL YOU SHUT *UP* FOR ONE SECOND?...

I'M TRYING TO *CONCENTRATE* HERE.

WHAT DO YOU MEAN, YOU'RE "TRYING TO CONCENTRATE"? WHAT'S WRONG?

I DUNNO... CAN'T SEEM TO KEEP IT TOGETHER...

I CAN'T MAKE MY RING WORK.

AS FOR *YOU,* FLASH... ANY ATTEMPT TO USE YOUR SUPERSPEED WILL BE *DETECTED,* CAUSING MOTION-SENSITIVE DETO- NATORS TO TRIGGER THE *BOMBS* I'VE BEEN PLANTING.

NO WAY.

OH MY GOD.

THAT'S BECAUSE YOUR THOUGHT PROCESSES ARE BEING *DISORGANIZED* BY SOMETHING I CALL *NEURAL CHAFF.*

67

TO BE CONTINUED...

OXYGEN PROCESSING:

HERE'S THE STORY SO FAR:

I REALLY HAVE TO TELL YOU HOW IMMENSELY *SATISFYING* THIS HAS BEEN.

STEEL WAS FIRST: I TOOK CONTROL OF HIS ARMOR AND COMMANDED IT TO TAKE HIM FOR A LONG WALK AND THEN TO TURN AROUND AND THROW HIS *HAMMER.*

THE FURTHER IT GOES, THE *HARDER* IT HITS. I BET YOU DIDN'T EVEN KNOW THAT.

THE *MARTIAN MANHUNTER'S* IN A STATE OF COMPLETE SPASTIC PARALYSIS--

UNABLE TO FORM A COHERENT PHYSICAL SHAPE. I USED A TOXIN WHICH STOPS HIS MOLECULES FROM FORMING POLYMER CHAINS.

I HAVE SOME MORE OF THAT FOR WHEN *PLASTIC MAN* SHOWS UP.

I KNOW A DOZEN WAYS TO DEFEAT EVERY SINGLE ONE OF YOU.

I HAVE DOSSIER FILES FOR EVERY "*SUPERHERO*" ON THE PLANET. I'VE BEEN PLANNING THIS.

WHO ARE YOU?

WHAT'S ALL THIS ABOUT? WHAT DID YOU SAY ABOUT MY SPEED AND *BOMBS* AND STUFF?

PROMETHEUS
UNBOUND

writer: GRANT MORRISON guest penciller: ARNIE JORGENSEN
guest inkers: DAVID MEIKIS and MARK PENNINGTON letterer: KEN LOPEZ colorist: PAT GARRAHY
separator: HEROIC AGE assistant editor: L.A. WILLIAMS editor: DAN RASPLER

AND AS FOR **YOU** TWO... "NEURAL CHAFF" I CALLED IT, GREEN LANTERN. IT DOESN'T WORK ON FLASH'S HIGH FREQUENCY BRAIN, BUT IT INTERFERES WITH **YOUR** BRAIN ELECTRICITY. IT'S LIKE GIVING YOUR THOUGHTS THE 'FLU.

SO MUCH FOR YOUR WILLPOWERED **RING.** RIGHT NOW YOU HAVE ALL THE WILLPOWER OF AN UNREPENTANT HEROIN ADDICT.

I SHOULD SHOOT YOU RIGHT NOW, PURELY OUT OF MERCY.

THERE.

I JUST DID.

HE SHOT ME.

WALLY.

WALLY HERE'S GOT TROUBLES OF HIS **OWN.**

REMEMBER. YOU MOVE ONE MOLECULE ABOVE NORMAL SPEED, WALLY, AND THOSE MOTION DETECTORS SEND A SIGNAL TO THOSE **BOMBS** I PLANTED AND...

BOOM!

SO STAY PUT.

PAFF

72

VILLAIN GALLERY:

LOOK OUT THERE!

KA-KOOM!

EVEN THE SHUTTLES HAVE BEEN *DISABLED.* THERE'S ONLY *ONE* WAY TO GET THESE PEOPLE OFF THE MOON, AND ONLY *I* KNOW IT.

PROMETHEUS.

BRAINS *AND* BRAWN. I'M IMPRESSED.

YOU KNOW, IT'S WEIRD HEARING *YOU* SAY THE NAME. IT'S LIKE I'VE ACTUALLY *MADE* IT. SUPERMAN SAID "PROMETHEUS" AND HE DIDN'T SOUND *SCARED.*

HE SHOULD BE. I'M HERE TO TAKE MY RIGHTFUL PLACE IN THIS GALLERY AS THE *GREATEST* SUPER-CRIMINAL OF ALL TIME.

THE ONE WHO *KILLED* THE JUSTICE LEAGUE.

AS SOON AS WE'VE SECURED THIS "PROMETHEUS", *YOU* CAN IMPART SOME OF YOUR SUPER-SPEED TO ACCELERATE GREEN LANTERN'S *METABOLISM.* THAT SHOULD ACCELERATE HIS NATURAL HEALING PROCESSES.

"SECURED"?

THE GUY WENT THROUGH US LIKE A HURRICANE, BATMAN.

HE KNOWS... *EVERYTHING* ABOUT ALL OF US. HE'S GOT FILES ON *EVERYBODY.*.

PLUS...NO *TELEPATHIC LINK*... MEANS HE REALLY DID TAKE *J'ONN* OUT.,.

FORTUNATELY, OUR *TECHNOLOGICAL* LINK IS STILL OPERATIONAL.

MEET THE JLA'S *SECRET MEMBER*, DATA *CENTRAL.*

ORACLE?

TROUBLE ON THE MOON.

WE'RE DEALING WITH AN INTRUDER WHO CALLS HIMSELF *"PROMETHEUS."* I THINK HE'S NEW, BUT RUN A FULL CROSS-REFERENCE ANYWAY.

IF WHAT HE'S SAYING IS TRUE, HE HAS THE SKILLS AND INGENUITY TO DEFEAT THE ENTIRE *JLA.* WE ALSO HAVE ONE HUNDRED CIVILIANS IN IMMEDIATE DANGER.

I'M TAKING THIS SERIOUSLY.

NOTHING ON FILE UNDER THAT NAME SO FAR, BATMAN. I'LL KEEP TRYING. I THINK S.T.A.R. LABS MIGHT HAVE A SHUTTLE THEY CAN SCRAMBLE, BUT IT'S GOING TO TAKE TIME...

RIGHT NOW YOU NEED A *MIRACLE.*

STEEL MEET EEL!

BE GENTLE WITH...

MMURRRKK!

PLASTIC MAN! THANK GOD!

RETURN.

HAK'K

FAPP

HERE'S THE UPDATE:

WE'RE UP AGAINST AN ICEMAN. HE'S A TECHNICAL GENIUS. HE'S HERE TO HURT PEOPLE.

BUT... IF WE CAN GET TO WITHIN A DOZEN FEET OF HIM, I CAN SEIZE CONTROL OF HIS TECHNOLOGY.

SURE! AND I'LL TRY TO SEIZE CONTROL OF MY DIGESTION.

LEAD THE WAY. I'LL SLINK ALONG BEHIND, COUGHING UP SPINE FRAGMENTS...

I'M SORRY, I...

CLARK, IF YOU CAN HEAR ME, SOMETHING WEIRD JUST HAPPENED HERE.

...WISH I COULD HAVE BEEN THERE TO HELP.

CAT ISN'T...

CAT ISN'T CAT.

SO YOU'RE JUST ANOTHER POOR LITTLE MOMMY'S BOY, IS *THAT* IT, PROMETHEUS?

NO, I HAD THAT DEALT WITH BY A REICHIAN THERAPIST IN VIENNA...

WHO...

MIAO, BABY.

LET ME TELL YOU SOMETHING ABOUT THE *BULLWHIP.*

AH.

WHHUTCH!

JUST SAVED YOU A LIFE, CATS.

NEXT ONE'S FOR YOU, PROMETHEUS.

THE HUNTRESS. RIGHT.

I FORGOT ABOUT YOU AFTER FIGHTING BATMAN...

TOO MUCH DATA FLOODING MY--

SHRRKKZZ

AOOWW!

AUWW! GOD! WHAT FAA...

YOUR ARMOR IS UNDER MY CONTROL...

THOKK!

THE ANGEL. DAMN!

FORGOT ABOUT YOU TOO.

BOTH AT THE SAME TIME.

WHAT HAVE YOU DONE TO--

MUST HAVE BEEN A BUG IN THE SHORT-TERM MEMORY.

KLIK

OUT.

ZAURIEL! ARE YOU?...

LIMBO! GREAT GOD... HIS HOUSE IS IN LIMBO...

ONLY THE DEAD GO THERE.

86

TAKION?

NOW *HIGHFATHER* OF *NEW GENESIS*, LIVING EMBODIMENT OF THE *ETERNAL SOURCE*.

THE WARRIORS *ORION* AND *BARDA* HAVE, UNTIL FURTHER NOTICE, BEEN ASSIGNED AS *PROTECTORS* OF EARTH.

WE CHOSE THOSE AMONG THE GODS WHOSE DISPOSITION MOST RESEMBLED THAT OF *HUMANKIND*.

AS *METRON'S* CALCULATIONS PREDICTED, NOW IT COMES TO PASS.

METRON TOLD US TO PREPARE FOR THE FORTIFICATION OF THE EARTH... AGAINST WHAT?

TAKION! WHAT DOES "ASSIGNED" AS "PROTECTORS" MEAN?

YOU WILL KNOW. THE NEW GODS MOVE IN MYSTERIOUS WAYS, SUPERMAN.

THEIR WONDERS TO PERFORM.

ORION, WHAT *IS* THIS? AN INVASION?

WE HAVE RULES HERE...

I AM A GOD OF *WAR*, SUPERMAN. I WILL FIGHT AND DIE IN YOUR PLANET'S DEFENSE IF THAT IS HIGHFATHER'S DECREE.

BUT I WILL NOT RECOGNIZE YOUR "RULES"! I WILL JUDGE AS *I* CHOOSE WHEN TO STRIKE AND WITH WHAT SEVERITY.

BOOM!

HH.

I'LL TRY MY BEST TO KEEP ORION CIVIL SUPERMAN.

WE MAY HAVE TO BRING *SOME* OF OUR MACHINES TO MAKE THE PLACE A LITTLE LESS... PRIMITIVE.

TRY TO LOOK ON IT AS A *TRANSFUSION*; OUR CULTURE HAS A LOT TO OFFER YOURS.

WE'RE GOING TO HAVE TO TALK, BARDA.

...I'VE BECOME OBSESSED WITH *COLLECTING* THINGS. I'VE GOT TO BE IN CHARGE OF THE TROPHY ROOM; IT'S THE ONLY WAY TO STOP MY OWN APARTMENT FROM FILLING UP WITH TRASH.

WHO'S THIS?

OKAY. IT'S HIM EXACTLY. BUT AFTER TODAY, I'M OFFICIALLY *PLASTIC MAN'S* BEST FRIEND IN THE WHOLE WORLD.

"I LOVE THIS PLACE. I LOVE THESE PEOPLE.

"EVERY DAY IS DOOMSDAY."

WE'VE JOINED A VERY INTERESTING GROUP, ZAURIEL. I'M LOOKING FORWARD TO SAVING THE EARTH ON A DAILY BASIS.

LADIES AND GENTLE-MEN.

IS THERE ANYONE LEFT WHO *ISN'T* A MEMBER OF THE *JLA*, SUPERMAN?

FORGET IT...

I UNDERSTAND YOUR RESERVATIONS, AQUAMAN, BUT AS FAR AS I'M CONCERNED, THE *JLA* HAS GROWN IN STRENGTH TODAY; WE ARE AT LAST THE FORCE FOR GOOD THAT WE DREAMED OF BECOMING.

I LOOK AROUND AND I SEE SOME OF THE GREATEST HEROES IN HISTORY, MEN AND WOMEN I'M *PROUD* TO STAND ALONGSIDE.

"AND IF *PROMETHEUS* IS ANY INDICATION OF THE KIND OF THREATS WE'RE GOING TO BE UP AGAINST, I THINK WE NEED ALL THE STRENGTH WE CAN GET...

"WE COULD HAVE *DIED* TODAY."

OUR NEW MEMBERS CAME THROUGH, AS WE KNEW THEY WOULD.

NOW, I'M AFRAID, THEY STILL HAVE ONE MORE ORDEAL *AHEAD*. THERE ARE ONE HUNDRED PEOPLE OUT THERE, WHO WANT NOTHING MORE THAN TO GET BACK TO SOMEWHERE WITH A RELIABLE *AIR* SUPPLY.

SO... THOSE OF YOU WHO WISH CAN FOLLOW ME TO THE RECEPTION AREA. BIG SMILES, PLEASE.

THE STRANGE CASE OF
Dr. JULIAN
SEPTEMBER

SEVEN WEEKS AGO.

I ALMOST FEEL **SORRY** FOR YOU, SON. YOU REALLY ARE AN **ILL-FATED** SONUVAGUN TO'VE DRAWN **ME** AS YOUR **EVALUATOR.**

JULIAN SEPTEMBER, PROFESSOR OF QUANTUM MECHANICS. CAN YOU FIX MY JEEP?

NOT THAT KIND OF **MECHANIC,** SIR.

TOO **BAD**...BECAUSE THAT'S THE **ONLY** WAY I'D HAVE **APPROVED** YOUR **COLOSSAL DRAIN** ON THE MILITARY GRANT BUDGET.

EXPECTING ME TO BELIEVE THAT **LUCK** COMES OUT OF A **MACHINE**...

THERE ARE **OTHERS** ON THE BOARD WHO'D **GIVE** YOU THIS GRANT. UNFORTUNATELY FOR **YOU,** I'M NOT ONE OF THEM.

CAN YOUR FANCY COMPUTER FIX **THAT,** PROFESSOR?

FUNDING GRANTED

FUNDING DENIED

LET'S **SEE.**

ENGAGED

ENGAGED

TAK

KRA KOOM!

...CONDOLENCES TO GENERAL VINSON'S **FAMILY,** SIRS. I'M SURE HE'S LOOKING DOWN UPON THIS MOMENT WITH... **WONDER.**

I'VE BEEN UNLUCKY ALL MY **LIFE,** BUT I CAN GUARANTEE YOU...

...THAT'S **ALL ABOUT** TO CHANGE...

AAAAAAH!

OH, RIGHT. I'M YOUR *RAFT.* LIKE I *ENJOY* BUTT CLEAVAGE IN MY FACE.

LET'S TAKE THIS LITTLE PARTY TO *SHORE.* WHO NEEDS A *HAND?* YOU, SIR, WITH THE *BEADY EYES*--

?

SPLOOSH

?

OR, IN THE WORDS OF THE GREAT SHAKE-SPEARE...

SHLORP

"?"

SHLOOP

BOYS? BOYS? WHATSAMATTA? YOU SLEEPIN' WITH THE *FISHES...?*

AQUADUDE! WHAT BRINGS *YOU* HERE, MY FINNY FRIEND?

ULP!

NOT THAT THERE'S ANYTHING *WRONG* WITH THAT...!

JUST IN THE *NEIGHBORHOOD*...WHICH, NOW THAT I *THINK* ABOUT IT, IS *STRANGE*...

...THOUGH NOT AS STRANGE AS *YOU*.

THANKS *AGAIN*... BUT HOW DOES THIS GET MARKED DOWN IN MY *JLA STATS*? DO I HAVE TO CREDIT YOU WITH AN *ASSIST*, OR--

IN THE *FIRST* PLACE, THERE *ARE* NO "STATS."

IN THE *SECOND* PLACE, HOW MUCH CREDIT DO YOU *WANT*?

YOU *DEFEATED* THEM LARGELY BECAUSE YOU BORE A STRIKING RESEMBLANCE TO THEIR *RAFT*.

DON'T I *KNOW* IT! WHAT A *COINKYDINK*, HUH? I MEAN--

AQUADUDE? WHERE YA *GOIN',* MAN? WAS IT SOMETHING I *SAID*...?

TONIGHT ON CHANNEL SEVEN NEWS: PHYSICIST JULIAN SEPTEMBER, AMERICA'S NEWEST NOBEL PRIZE WINNER...

GOTHAM CITY.

HE'LL *KILL* US! FOR GOD'S SAKE, *BRUCE,* WHERE'S THE *HATCH?*

INTERIOR *ESCAPE HATCHES* ON ELEVATORS ARE A THING OF *MOVIES* AND *TELEVISION.* THOSE ON *MODERN* ELEVATORS CAN BE ACCESSED ONLY FROM *OUTSIDE* THE CAR. HE'S GOT US *TRAPPED.*

NO! THERE *HAS* TO BE A WAY *OUT!*

THERE *ISN'T* ONE, *KNIPKE.*

I'M *THINKING,* RANDOLPH...

...I'M *THINKING.*

YOU *HEAR* ME, *WAYNE?* KISS YOUR ASSETS *GOODBYE,* YOU RICH *FOP!* MY WIFE TOOK THE *KIDS,* AN' IT'S *YOUR FAULT!*

I DI'N *DESERVE* TO BE FIRED! I'M A *GOOD GUY!* THERE'S NOTHIN' *WRONG* WITH *ME!*

THERE'S NOTHIN' *WRONG* WITH ME!

CLEARLY.

FIFTEEN SECONDS, WAYNE!

OH, *GOD,* BRUCE! GIVE HIM HIS JOB BACK! DO *SOMETHING!*

I *INTEND* TO.

96

NEWARK.

TURN...

...TURN...

...TURN!

WONDER WOMAN TO SUPERMAN! THAT'S TWO! HOW MANY MORE ARE CONVERGING ON THE SAME AIRSPACE?

BELIEVE IT OR NOT-- FIVE.

I'VE GOT THE NEXT THREE. JUST AS I'M CONVERTING MY VOICE INTO AN ELECTRO-MAGNETIC FREQUENCY YOU CAN HEAR--

--I CAN CUT INTO THE RADIO SIGNALS THAT MANIPULATE THEIR WINGFLAPS!

STEEL? EEL, WHAT ST BLEW?

ENGINE NUMBER TWO ON THE 7:07 FROM *CHICAGO*. ONLY WAY I *HAD* TO SHIFT ITS *TRAJECTORY* IN TIME.

THE POOR *PASSENGERS* ARE SWALLOWING THEIR *PEANUTS* HARD--BUT THEY'LL LIMP OKAY TO THE *TARMAC*. MEET YOU THERE!

NICELY *DONE*. HEPHAESTUS *HIMSELF* WOULD BE PROUD.

YEAH, WELL, TELL HIM I SAID *HELLO*, I GUESS.

FUNNY, I DON'T NORMALLY SCAN THE ATC BANDS.* I STUMBLED ONTO *THIS* MESS PURELY BY *COINCIDENCE*.

* AIR TRAFFIC CONTROL--EDITOR.

SOMEHOW, A *COMPUTER GLITCH* MAPPED *SEVEN JUMBO JETS* ON AN *IDENTICAL FLIGHT PATH*.

THE ODDS ON *THAT* ARE...

WHAT THE...? WHAT'S WITH THE *NEWSPAPERS*?

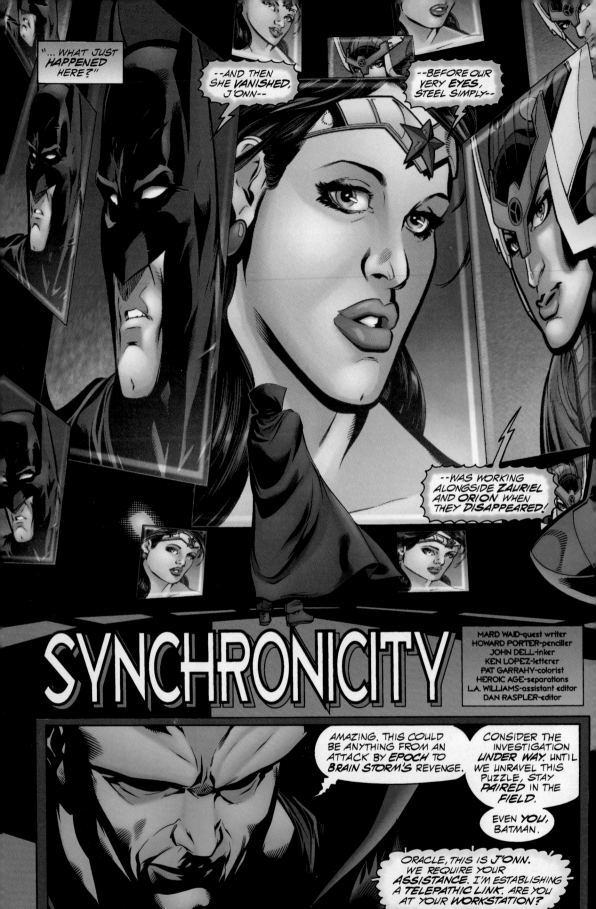

SYNCHRONICITY

MARD WAID-guest writer
HOWARD PORTER-penciller
JOHN DELL-inker
KEN LOPEZ-letterer
PAT GARRAHY-colorist
HEROIC AGE-separations
L.A. WILLIAMS-assistant editor
DAN RASPLER-editor

I'M SERIOUS! BY PURE COINCIDENCE, ALL SEVEN PICKED THIS MOMENT TO STRIKE! NOW THEY'RE MADDER AT EACH OTHER THAN THEY ARE AT US--

--AND IT'S ALL WE CAN DO TO PULL BYSTANDERS OUT OF THEIR CROSSFIRE! SEND REINFORCEMENTS FAST, BEFORE--

ORACLE, WHAT ARE THE ODDS OF SEVEN SUPER-VILLAINS ATTACKING THE WHITE HOUSE INDEPENDENTLY?

TELEPORTER: ACTIVATE.

EVEN IN OUR WORLD, OFF THE CHARTS. I'LL CALL IN THE TROOPS--

PARDON ME.

COMIN' THROUGH.

THIS WAY, MA'AM. GOTTA GET YOU OUT OF THE HOT ZONE!

"MA'AM"?

LINDA? WHY AREN'T YOU AT HOME? WHAT ARE YOU DOING HERE?

FLEW IN FOR A PRESS CONFERENCE, SWEETIE. SMALL WORLD.

NOT SMALL ENOUGH. DIDN'T GL RING FOR THE CAVALRY? WHERE'S THE BACKUP? WHERE'S THE--

WHEW!!

ARE WE AT *FULL FORCE?* WHERE IS *THE BATMAN?* WHO WAS LAST *WITH* HIM?

OH, THAT'S RIGHT. YOU'RE *NEW* TO THE TEAM.

YOU ACTUALLY *EXPECTED* HIM TO PARTNER UP.

WOULDN'T HE JUST BE *UNDERFOOT*?

LISTEN TO THE *OTHER* NEW GUY.

ARE YOU *KIDDING*? WHO ELSE BUT *BATMAN* IS GONNA EXPLAIN WHY THE *WORLD'S* GONE WACK?

¡NNNGH!

BARDA! LOOK *OUT*! THIS IS THE *OVAL OFFICE*!

THOOM!

WE MUST PROTECT THE *PRESIDENT* FROM--

BARDA!

WONDER *WOMAN*! WHERE'D SHE *GO*? I'M UNDER *FULL ATTACK* HERE!

NO MATTER. YOU CAN HANDLE IT. GUESS I'M *LUCKY* THE *JLA* CAME ALONG.

?

JULIAN SEPTEMBER? THE MAN IN THE *NEWSPAPER*?

ON *TELEVISION*?

J'ONN? ORACLE. I WAS JUST *READING* ABOUT HIM--A QUANTUM PHYSICIST WHO SAYS HE DISCOVERED "THE BUILDING BLOCKS OF PROBABILITY."

CLAIMS HE CHANCED UPON A WAY TO MANIPULATE *COINCIDENCE* ON A *SUB-ATOMIC* LEVEL. SOMETHING ABOUT A *PHOTON* EXPERIMENT...? HOW DOES THAT TRANSLATE INTO THE *PRESIDENCY?*

WE'RE *ABOUT TO* ASK.

FORCEFULLY.

SIR, WE HAVE A *STRONG FEELING* YOU DON'T BELONG HERE.

YOU...YOU *KNOW...?*

IF YOU'LL COME WITH *US...*

THAT'S...NOT *POSSIBLE.*

BEHOLD--THE *ENGINE OF CHANCE!* WITH IT AT MY *SIDE,* PROBABILITY IS *ALWAYS* IN MY FAVOR!

LET ME *SHOW* YOU! AT MY *COMMAND,* THE ODDS OF AN *EARTHQUAKE* RIPPING THROUGH *WASHINGTON'S BEDROCK*--

"--HAVE SUDDENLY BECOME BETTER THAN EVEN!"

J'ONN, TAKE HIM **OUT!** WHATEVER HE'S DOING TO THE **PROBABILITY FIELD,** HE JUST CRANKED UP THE **VOLUME!**

IMPOSSIBLY ENOUGH, THE **SUDAN** HAS GONE **DRY--**

"--WHILE A **TSUNAMI** JUST SWAMPED **MOBILE, ALABAMA** FOR THE FIRST TIME IN **HISTORY,** AND--"

"--OH, GOOD LORD--"

"--SEVEN OF **TOKYO'S** TALLEST SKYSCRAPERS HAVE BURST INTO **FLAME!**"

"I CAN'T POSSIBLY **PREDICT** WHAT COULD HAPPEN **NEXT,** J'ONN! FOR GOD'S SAKE-- **CLOCK HIM!**"

108

SEPTEMBER, STOP! THE FORCES YOU'RE UNLEASHING-- THEY'RE TEARING THE WORLD APART!

AND PUTTING IT BACK IN AN ORDER I LIKE! ALL MY LIFE, I'VE BEEN UNLUCKY! NO MORE!

"LUCKY"? SEVEN BAD GUYS SHOWED UP TO SMOOSH YOU!

"AND THE MIGHTY JLA ARRIVED TO SAVE ME! DON'T YOU SEE?

"IT'LL ALL BENEFIT ME! IT ALWAYS DOES!"

YOU CAN'T TAKE ME DOWN! I AM FORTUNE'S CHILD!

THAK

...AND THAT'S WHERE WE *ARE*. THANKS TO SOMETHING SEPTEMBER PUT IN *MOTION*, THE LAWS OF *PROBABILITY* ARE BREAKING DOWN BEFORE OUR *EYES*.

WE THOUGHT HIS *ENGINE OF CHANCE* WAS THE CAUSE...BUT THAT'S *SHATTERED*, AND THE CRISIS IS STILL *BUILDING*.

AT FIRST, THIS PROBABILITY FLUX WAS CONFINED TO THE PRESENT. NOW IT SEEMS IT'S STRETCHING INTO THE *PAST*. SOMEONE *ELSE* WON THE *PRESIDENCY*, FOR INSTANCE...

...WHILE OTHER HISTORICAL IMPROBABILITIES ARE OCCURRING *FASTER* AND *FASTER*, AS IF IN A *CHAIN REACTION*.

THEY CAN ONLY GET WORSE FROM *HERE*.

HOW *MUCH* WORSE? *COLUMBUS-NEVER-FOUND-AMERICA* WORSE?

SNAKE RIVER? SEVENTH FLOOR JUMBO JETS

THINK *DEEPER*. SUPPOSE THE *BIG BANG* NEVER *HAPPENED*.

SUPPOSE *CLAUDIA SCHIFFER* NEVER MARRIED *DAVID COPPERFIELD!*

SUPPOSE--*HEY!* SUPPOSE *WE'RE* BEING *RETROACTIVELY ERASED!* THAT'S WHAT'S HAPPENED TO *BARDA*, RIGHT?

ANY *SECOND* NOW, *WE* COULD VANISH! THE LIGHTNING THAT TURNED *WALLY* INTO THE *FLASH* COULD NEVER HAVE *STRUCK*--

-- OR SOMEONE *ELSE* COULD HAVE GOTTEN THE *GREEN LANTERN* RING! SEPTEMBER'S BEHIND *THAT*, TOO!

WRONG. BARDA'S DISAPPEARANCE *SURPRISED* HIM, REMEMBER?

OKAY, SEE, THIS IS WHY IF YOU'RE NOT AROUND TO EXPLAIN THINGS, WE'RE *SCREWED*. HOW CAN IT NOT BE *SEPTEMBER'S* FAULT? HOW BIG A COINCIDENCE IS *THAT*?

IT'S *MORE* THAN COINCIDENCE. BE MORE *OBSERVANT*. OUR RANKS HAVE BEEN *WINNOWED*...

DOES THAT NUMBER STRIKE A CHORD WITH EVERYONE? I THOUGHT SO.

WORLDWIDE, THE NUMBER *SEVEN* IS COMING INTO PLAY WITH ALARMING *FREQUENCY*. PLASTIC MAN, YOU ENCOUNTERED *AQUAMAN* AT *SNAKE RIVER*...

...OR, MORE *PRECISELY*, *SEVEN DEVILS CANYON*.

OOOH, GOOD ONE.

SO?

...TO SEVEN.

I HAD MY *OWN* ENCOUNTER WITH *SEVENS* THIS EVENING... AS DID *SUPERMAN* AND *WONDER WOMAN*, WHO PREVENTED THE COLLISION OF *SEVEN* AIRPLANES.

EVEN *JULIAN SEPTEMBER* IS A SEVEN OF SORTS JULIAN SUGGESTS *JULY*, THE SEVENTH MONTH...

...WHILE *SEPTEMBER* WAS THE SEVENTH CYCLE OF THE ANCIENT ROMAN CALENDAR.

IT'S CALLED *SYNCHRONICITY:* THE CONVERGENCE OF *RELATED* EVENTS.

A *PHONE CALL* OUT OF THE BLUE FROM SOMEONE MOMENTS AFTER YOU *THINK* OF THEM. AN OLD *SONG* HEARD THREE TIMES IN ONE *DAY.*

AND FOR *US...* A *NUMBER* THAT SURFACES AGAIN AND *AGAIN.*

SO WHAT DOES IT *MEAN?*

FOR STARTERS, IT MEANS THERE'LL BE NO MORE *DISAPPEAR-ANCES.* IF MY THEORY *HOLDS,* WE'RE *STABLE* AT *SEVEN* MEMBERS.

THEORY?

SEE WHAT I MEAN? PREPARE TO BE *DAZZLED.*

HE *ALWAYS* HAS *ALL* THE ANSWERS. DON'T KNOW WHAT WE'D DO *WITHOUT* HIM.

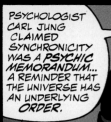

PSYCHOLOGIST CARL JUNG CLAIMED SYNCHRONICITY WAS A *PSYCHIC MEMORANDUM...* A REMINDER THAT THE UNIVERSE HAS AN UNDERLYING *ORDER.*

I'M NOT SURE I BUY *INTO* THAT...BUT I *DO* ACCEPT THAT *FATE* OR *CHANCE* OR THE *UNIVERSE* IS *USING* SYNCHRONICITY TO TELL US SOMETHING *CRITICAL* ABOUT WHAT SEPTEMBER HAS *DONE...* AND WHAT HAS TO BE PUT *RIGHT.*

THE SEVENS ARE *A MESSAGE...* AND THEY MEAN

BATMAN?

NEXT: THINGS GET WORSE

SEVEN HOURS AGO, IT BEGAN.

JUSTICE LEAGUERS STARTED *VANISHING*, SEEMINGLY AT *RANDOM*...

...WHILE, AROUND THE WORLD, *PROBABILITY* WENT *WILD*.

DESPITE THE ODDS AGAINST IT, *SEVEN* JUMBO JETS CROSSED FLIGHT *PATHS*. SEVEN *TOKYO* SKY-SCRAPERS SIMUL-TANEOUSLY BURST INTO *FLAME*.

GLOBAL *CATASTROPHE* CAME IN SEVENS AND *MORE SEVENS*...

...AS THE *JUSTICE LEAGUE* BATTLED *JULIAN SEPTEMBER* AND HIS *ODDSBREAK-ING ENGINE OF CHANCE.*

WITH SEPTEMBER *DEFEATED*, THE REMAINING LEAGUERS BELIEVED THE *CATACLYSM* WOULD *END.*

INSTEAD, THE *PANDEMONIUM* SEPTEMBER PUT IN MOTION SOMEHOW RACED *ONWARD*... *BENDING* BACK THROUGH *TIME ITSELF*...

...*CHANGING* THE OUTCOME OF *HISTORICAL EVENTS*...

...*TWISTING IMPROBABILITY* INTO *CERTAINTY*...

...LEAVING *SEVEN JLAERS* ADRIFT IN A *WORLD*...

...WHERE ANYTHING IS POSSIBLE.

GOTHAM GAZETTE ON THE WEB

Today's Headlines: Society

MILLIONAIRE BRUCE WAYNE RETURNS FROM YEARS ABROAD

AS A BOY: Mugger's gun misfires; chance blessing buys Wayne family, Gotham, many prosperous years

SEVEN SOLDIERS OF PROBABILITY

MARK WAID-guest writer
HOWARD PORTER-penciller
JOHN DELL & WALDEN WONG-inkers
KEN LOPEZ-letterer
PAT GARRAHY-colorist
HEROIC AGE-separations
L.A. WILLIAMS-ass't editor
DAN RASPLER-editor

WASHINGTON.

BATMAN WAS RIGHT *HERE!* NOW THERE'S NO *SIGN* OF HIM! HE VANISHED, *TOO!*

I DON'T *GET* IT! HE SAID THAT SOME KINDA *COSMIC JUJU* WAS PARING THE TEAM DOWN TO *SEVEN*--BUT *WITHOUT* HIM, WE'RE DOWN TO--

--SEVEN *EXACTLY*, GREEN LANTERN. I'M IN TELEPATHIC COMMUNICATION WITH *ORACLE.*

IN FACT, SHE'S RELAYING A DISCREET *SHORTWAVE* MESSAGE TO YOU, SUPERMAN. YOUR ENERGY POWERS SHOULD ALLOW YOU TO HEAR IT...

--I SAID PROBABILITY HAS SHIFTED *HISTORY--AGAIN!* DON'T TELL THE *OTHERS*--THEY DON'T KNOW BATMAN'S *REAL IDENTITY*--

--BUT OUR DARK KNIGHT NO LONGER *EXISTS*--BECAUSE THE GUN THAT KILLED HIS PARENTS *MISFIRED!*

THAT MADE ALL THE *DIFFERENCE!* REMEMBER, BRUCE'S WHOLE LIFE WAS *CHANGED* BY THE COURSE OF TWO...

...BULLETS...

SO WE'RE *SEVEN*... AND BATMAN SAID *SEVEN* WAS SOME SORT OF *MESSAGE.* BUT WHAT DOES IT *MEAN?*

I DON'T *KNOW*, BUT WE'D BETTER FIND OUT *FAST*, BEFORE ANYTHING ELSE GOES...

...FLOOEY...

WHAT THE...?

WOW! CONGRATULATIONS, SUPES...

ORACLE'S NOT *RESPONDING?*

FINE. HOW MUCH INFO DO WE *NEED?* WE *KNOW* WHO'S *RESPONSIBLE--SEPTEMBER!*

NO. REMEMBER, BATMAN SAID THIS *WASN'T* HIS DOING --AT LEAST, NOT *DIRECTLY.*

ONCE SEPTEMBER BEGAN MANIPULATING THE LAWS OF CHANCE FOR HIS OWN GAIN, THE UNIVERSE BEGAN PLAYING A *COUNTERGAME* WITH *PROBABILITY.*

BATMAN CALLED IT *SYNCHRONICITY--* THE *CONVERGENCE* OF *RELATED EVENTS.* IN *OUR* CASE, AN ONGOING SEQUENCE OF *SEVENS.*

HOWEVER, UNTIL WE DETERMINE THEIR *SIGNIFICANCE,* SEPTEMBER IS STILL OUR *PREY.*

SO HOW DO YOU SUGGEST WE *FIND* HIM?

I HAVE MY WAYS. I AM, AFTER ALL, A *MANHUNTER.*

?

ALL THOSE WHO'VE EVER SEEN J'ONN *ANGRY,* RAISE THEIR *HANDS...?* THAT'S WHAT I *THOUGHT.*

WHAT MADE HIM *MAD?*

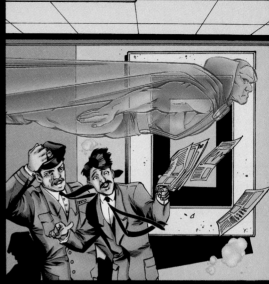

FILE
ROOM
Security
Clearance
A-1
ONLY

September, Julian
Security Clearance
Required

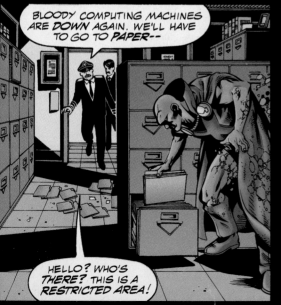

BLOODY COMPUTING MACHINES ARE *DOWN* AGAIN. WE'LL HAVE TO GO TO *PAPER*--

HELLO? WHO'S *THERE?* THIS IS A *RESTRICTED AREA!*

AS WELL IT *SHOULD* BE.

YOUR MAJESTY--?

GIVE ME EVERYTHING WE *HAVE* ON THIS MAN AND HIS LIKELY *WHEREABOUTS--* IMMEDIATELY.

BRING!
BRING!

THIS IS BARBARA GORDON. I CAN'T COME TO THE PHONE RIGHT NOW. LEAVE A MESSAGE. ⊰BEEP⊱

BARBARA? ARE YOU SCREENING?

BARBARA, THIS IS BRUCE. IT'S BEEN AGES. I'M STOPPING BY TO SEE YOU. HOPE YOU'RE THERE.

I'M BRINGING MOM AND DAD WITH ME...

IS IT MONSOON SEASON ALREADY? I DIDN'T SEND OUT ANY CARDS--!

ALL THE HIGH TIDES ARE OUT OF CONTROL, PLASTIC MAN!

THAT'S WHAT HAPPENS WHEN THE WORLD STARTS SPINNING *FASTER!*

AS IF THINGS COULDN'T GET ANY *WORSE*--THERE ARE SUDDENLY *SEVEN HOURS* IN A *DAY!*

WHAT? THE EARTH CAN'T TAKE THAT KIND OF *STRAIN!*

NEITHER CAN *I.* I WISH *J'ONN* WERE HERE. BATMAN PROMISED WE'D STAY *STEADY* AT *SEVEN MEMBERS*--

--BUT MAYBE HE VANISHED *ANYWAY* AND--*WAIT!* HE'S SENDING A *SIGNAL!*

"IF HE'S LOCATED *SEPTEMBER*--"

--THEN THIS CASE IS FINALLY WRAPPED *UP!*

BY NOW, J'ONN'S PROBABLY USED *TELEPATHY* TO FERRET OUT WHATEVER *SEPTEMBER*--

--*KNOWS*--

EESH.

THE MYSTERY IS FAR FROM *SOLVED.* THE LAWS OF CHANCE *CONTINUE* TO BEND AND BREAK TO OUR *DISADVANTAGE.*

I FOUND *JULIAN SEPTEMBER.* A YOUNG MAN IN EXCELLENT HEALTH. NON-*SMOKER,* NON-*DRINKER.*

DEAD OF A HEART ATTACK AT AGE *TWENTY-SIX.*

SO MUCH FOR THE *INTERROGATION.* HOWZABOUT ALL THESE *COMPUTERS?* THEY MUST KNOW *SOMETHING...*

SEPTEMBER'S *COMPUTER* FILES ARE *ENCRYPTED.* J'ONN, CAN ORACLE *DECODE* THEM?

ORACLE, THIS IS *J'ONN.*

J'ONN, NOT *NOW,* NOT--

NOW. NO THANKS TO *YOU,* WE'VE LOCATED *SEPTEMBER*-- TOO LATE.

DON'T TAKE THAT TONE WITH ME, *J'ONN.* I'M--

--GAMBLING THE FATE OF THE *WORLD* AGAINST YOUR *PERSONAL* GAIN!

MY DISAPPOINTMENT IN YOU IS *LIMITLESS!* HOW *DARE* YOU? YOU *WITHDREW* FROM THIS CASE HOPING THAT HISTORY WOULD *CONTINUE* TO CHANGE--

--AND *ERASE* THE GUNSHOTS THAT *SHATTERED* YOUR *SPINE!*

I AM-- --WRONG! SO THAT'S WHAT YOU THINK OF ME, J'ONN? GOOD GOD. MY HESITATION HAS NOTHING TO DO WITH ME!

YOU'RE ASKING ME TO PULL A TRIGGER!

TRIGGER--?

ON THE WAYNES, J'ONN! FOR THE FIRST TIME IN HIS TORTURED LIFE, BRUCE WAYNE IS AT PEACE! HIS PARENTS DIDN'T DIE! WE CAN'T JUST DISREGARD THAT!

WHY DID I WITHDRAW? I'VE BEEN BUSY CRUNCHING THE ODDS--TRYING TO FIND SOME WAY TO PRESERVE THEIR SAFETY ONCE WE SET THINGS RIGHT!

J'ONN, YOU DON'T KNOW WHAT IT'S LIKE TO FEEL A BULLET VIOLATE YOUR BODY. TO PULP FLESH AND BONE. I DO.

TO KNOWINGLY LET THAT HAPPEN TO THE WAYNES... IT WOULDN'T BE HUMA--

--I MEAN--

I KNOW WHAT YOU MEAN.

LET SUPERMAN'S POWERS READ THE FILES. I'M WORKING WITH SOME PROBABILITY TABLES. IF I CAN--

WE HAVEN'T TIME! BARBARA, WE'RE BOTH ANALYTICAL THINKERS!

YOU KNOW THIS IS A FOOL'S ERRAND! YOU'RE USING IT AS AN EXCUSE NOT TO MAKE A HARD CHOICE!

WELL, BEING IN THE JLA IS ABOUT MAKING HARD CHOICES.

YOUR HEART IS STRONG, BARBARA...BUT YOUR MIND IS EVEN STRONGER. GO WITH IT.

WELL? CAN SHE HELP?

I DON'T KNOW IF SHE WILL OR--

WE'RE IN! ORACLE UNLOCKED THE FILES--

--BUT THEY'RE INCOMPREHENSIBLE! WHAT'S ALL THIS STUFF ABOUT SUBATOMIC PARTICLES?

NONE OF US ARE *PHYSICISTS.* WE ARE SO *CLOSE,* BUT WITHOUT ANYONE TO *INTERPRET* SEPTEMBER'S DATA, WE REMAIN--

--LOST--

J'ONN? HE'S *FADING!*

NO! HOW CAN THIS *BE?* SEVEN MEMBERS WAS OUR *CONSTANT!*

SEVEN... SEVEN...

OF *COURSE.* LISTEN TO ME!

WHEN THE *ATOM* ARRIVES, YOU MUST TELL HIM *EVERYTHING!*

EVERYthing--

THE *ATOM?* RAY *PALMER?* RAY IS A *SCIENTIST,* BUT--

--BUT HE'S NOT *HERE*--AND WE'LL *NEVER* FIND HIM IN TIME TO--

RING! RING!

WOW. IS *THIS* A WRONG NUMBER!

I WAS TRYING TO PHONE *HOME*. SOMEBODY WANT TO FILL ME IN ON WHERE I *AM*?

HOW DID J'ONN *KNOW* HE'D--?

SEARCH ME.

...AND THAT'S ALL WE KNOW.

LET *ME* TAKE A LOOK. MAYBE I CAN...

UH-OH.

"UH-OH"?

BATMAN WAS *RIGHT.* THE SEVENS ARE A *POINTER*--AND YOU WON'T *BELIEVE* WHAT THEY'RE POINTING *TO.*

OKAY. IF I WERE GOING TO STORE A *PHOTON*, WHERE WOULD I--?

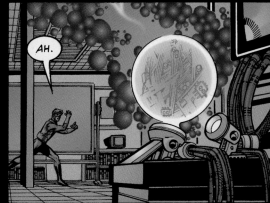

AH.

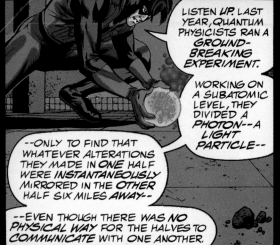

LISTEN *UP.* LAST YEAR, QUANTUM PHYSICISTS RAN A *GROUNDBREAKING* EXPERIMENT.

WORKING ON A SUBATOMIC LEVEL, THEY DIVIDED A *PHOTON*--A *LIGHT PARTICLE*--

--ONLY TO FIND THAT WHATEVER ALTERATIONS THEY MADE IN *ONE* HALF WERE *INSTANTANEOUSLY* MIRRORED IN THE *OTHER* HALF SIX MILES *AWAY*--

--EVEN THOUGH THERE WAS *NO PHYSICAL WAY* FOR THE HALVES TO *COMMUNICATE* WITH ONE ANOTHER.

COINCIDENCE?

QUITE THE *OPPOSITE.* IT SUGGESTED THAT THERE *IS* NO COINCIDENCE...

...BUT, RATHER, A HERETOFORE-UNSEEN *INTERDEPENDENCE* BETWEEN *ALL* EVENTS. AN *INVISIBLE WEB* TYING *EVERYTHING* TOGETHER.

AN UNDERLYING *ORDER* TO THE *UNIVERSE.*

A *SYNCHRONICITY.*

PRECISELY.

STAND HERE AND POINT.

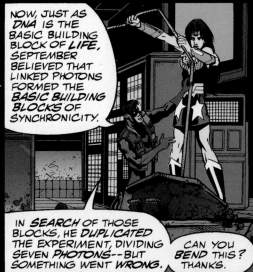

NOW, JUST AS *DNA* IS THE BASIC BUILDING BLOCK OF *LIFE,* SEPTEMBER BELIEVED THAT LINKED PHOTONS FORMED THE *BASIC BUILDING BLOCKS* OF SYNCHRONICITY.

IN *SEARCH* OF THOSE BLOCKS, HE *DUPLICATED* THE EXPERIMENT, DIVIDING SEVEN *PHOTONS*--BUT SOMETHING WENT *WRONG.*

CAN YOU *BEND* THIS? THANKS.

WHEN HIS *COMPUTER PROGRAM* GLITCHED, HE DID THE *AMAZING.* HE INADVERTENTLY *DESTROYED* HIS PHOTONS' *LINK*--

--AND IN *DOING SO,* POISONED THE NATURAL ORDER OF *REALITY.*

WORKING *THAT SMALL?* HOW DO YOU GET FROM *SCREWED-UP* PHOTONS TO COLLIDING *JUMBO JETS?*

SEVEN PAIRS OF *HALF-PHOTONS.* REJOINING THEM IS THE ONLY WAY TO NULLIFY *UNIVERSAL CHAOS.*

WAIT. I'M CONFUSED. IF WE'RE SMALLER THAN *LIGHT* PARTICLES NOW, HOW ARE WE EVEN *SEEING?*

YOU CAN OPEN YOUR *EYES* NOW. THERE THEY *ARE.*

BY THE WAY, YOU'RE NOT BREATHING *OXYGEN,* EITHER.

IT'S BEST NOT TO THINK ABOUT IT.

YOU'RE *NOT...* NOT IN ANY *HUMAN* WAY. THE FIVE SENSES BECOME SOMETHING ELSE *ENTIRELY* AT THIS QUANTUM LEVEL.

YOUR MIND'S DOING YOU A *FAVOR.* IT'S PROCESSING ALL THIS INTO *FAMILIAR VISUALS* SO YOU WON'T GO INSANE.

NO KIDDING.

BY CLICKING THE BUTTON IN THE PALM OF MY *GLOVE*, I CAN INCREASE MY *MASS*--

--STEER THIS HALF-PHOTON TOWARDS ITS *MATE*--

--AND PUT THEM BACK *TOGETHER!*

AT THE *SPEED* THEY'RE MOVING, THEY'RE *DIFFICULT* TO *LASSO*--

--BUT IF WE'RE LEARNING *ANYTHING* TODAY-- IT'S THAT *NOTHING* IS *IMPOSSIBLE!*

PLEASE, GOD... I DON'T THINK I CAN BEAR TO SEE WHO'S COMING THROUGH THE DOOR.

--CHANGGGHAAA!

THE PROBABILITY CANCER-- IT'S FIGHTING BACK!

IT'S ALTERED HISTORY SO THAT SOMEONE ELSE RECEIVED THE GREEN LANTERN RING!

WORSE--GOOD LORD-- IT'S CHANGED WALLY SO THAT THE ELECTRIFIED CHEMICALS THAT ONCE GAVE HIM SUPER-SPEED--

AIEEEEE!

--INSTEAD BURNED HIM TO THE BONE!

TAP TAP TAP TAP

TIME'S RUNNING OUT FAST, SUPERMAN.

WITH EVERY CLOCKTICK, THE PROBABILITY OF YOUR ROCKETSHIP HAVING LANDED IN A VOLCANO SOMEWHERE MULTIPLIES!

IN ORDER TO REPAIR THE LAST PHOTON--

BARBARA?

WHY...
WHY AM I
HERE...?

BARBARA, IS
SOMETHING
WRONG?

...
NO.

"NOT
ANYMORE."

WE'RE BACK-- BUT DID WE
SUCCEED? IS EVERYTHING
AS IT SHOULD BE?

ASK
THEM.

SEVEN VANISHED JLAERS.

--PRESENT AND ACCOUNTED FOR, FLASH. WHATEVER YOU DID--

--YOU DID IT WELL.

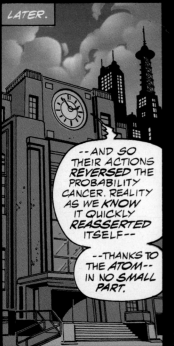

LATER.

--AND SO THEIR ACTIONS REVERSED THE PROBABILITY CANCER. REALITY AS WE KNOW IT QUICKLY REASSERTED ITSELF--

--THANKS TO THE ATOM-- IN NO SMALL PART.

FUNNY. BUT HOW DID YOU KNOW HE'D REPLACE YOU AS ONE OF THE SEVEN?

I DIDN'T--NOT FOR CERTAIN. I WAS, IF YOU'LL FORGIVE THE EXPRESSION, PLAYING THE ODDS.

OF ALL THE JLAERS TO HAVE SERVED THE TEAM IN ITS DECADE-LONG EXISTENCE, THE ATOM--

--WAS THE SEVENTH TO JOIN.

I APOLOGIZE FOR MISJUDG-ING YOUR MOTIVES, BARBARA. CLEARLY, WE DO NOT GIVE YOU ENOUGH CONSIDERATION.

THE LEAGUE IS CAPABLE OF BUILDING A WATCHTOWER ON THE MOON, SURELY WE COULD ENGINEER A PROSTHESIS FOR YOUR LEGS...

THANK YOU, BUT NO. I HAVE LITTLE INTEREST IN BEING HALF-ROBOT.

YOU DO MISS YOUR MOBILITY...?

MORE THAN WORDS CAN EXPRESS. AND I DREAM OF THE MEDICAL BREAK-THROUGHS THAT MIGHT SOMEDAY RESTORE IT.

BUT IN THE MEANTIME, I'VE WORKED HARD TO TREAT WHAT HAPPENED TO ME AS AN OPPOR-TUNITY, NOT A HANDICAP.

I CONCENTRATE ON THE GOOD I CAN DO NOW THAT I'VE BEEN FORCED TO EXERCISE MY MIND.

DESPITE HIS EVIL, J'ONN, SEPTEMBER HAD THE RIGHT NOTION.

"SOMETIMES OUR ONLY COMFORT COMES FROM BELIEVING THAT THERE IS NO CHANCE.

"THAT WHATEVER HAPPENS IN THIS WORLD...

WAYNE
THOMAS AND MARTHA
BELOVED PARENTS

"...HAPPENS FOR A REASON."

THE END

MYSTERY IN SPACE

JLA
WATCHTOWER.

WHERE I COME FROM, WE HAVE LITTLE USE FOR *TOYS*.

THEY'RE NOT *TOYS*, ORION. THEY'RE *TROPHIES*. OF *PAST BATTLES*. SURELY YOU CAN RESPECT *THAT*.

AND I KNOW I'M RISKING MY *TEETH* BY *TALKING* TO YOU LIKE THIS, BUT BE *CAREFUL* ABOUT WHAT YOU *TOUCH*.

YOU DON'T WANT TO BREACH THE *WALLS* ON A *MOONBASE*, AND YOU CAN NEVER TELL WHEN SOME-THING MIGHT STILL BE--

--LOADED--!

CHOOM!

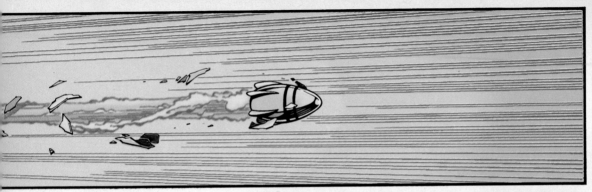

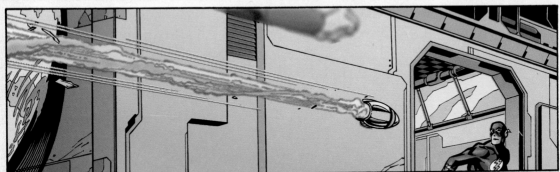

WHAT THE--?

OH, IT'S YOU!

PLEASE... BE MY GUEST!

THWOOM

HI. REMEMBER ME?

... I DIDN'T DO IT. IT WAS ORION.

HE DOESN'T *CARE,* LANTERN.

HEY, EVERYBODY-- GATHER 'ROUND! LOOK WHO'S *BACK*--AND FASTER THAN A SPEEDING *MORTAR!*

--CLOTHED IN THE FAMILIAR RED-AND-BLUE FOR *GOOD.* ONCE AFTER I HELPED RID THE WORLD OF THE MILLENIUM GIANTS, MY ELECTROMAGNETIC ENERGY DISPERSED-- RETURNING ME TO NORMAL.*

FRONT PAGE NEWS IN THE *DAILY PLANET.* WHAT IS IT WITH YOU AND THAT *KENT* GUY THAT HE'S ALWAYS BREAKING YOUR *NEWS?*

*IN *SUPERMAN FOREVER.*

WHO--? LATER. WE'RE ON *RANN?* ADAM, WHAT'S GOING *ON* HERE? HAVE YOU LOST YOUR *MIND?* YOU'VE ALWAYS BEEN AN *ALLY!*

RELEASE US *IMMEDIATELY!*

NOT A *CHANCE,* SUPERMAN. YOU AND THE LEAGUERS HAVE QUITE A TASK *AHEAD* OF YOU.

UNDER THE WATCH OF THE *EN'TARAN SLAVEMASTERS,* YOU WILL OBEY MY *EVERY COMMAND*--UNLESS YOU'D LIKE ANOTHER TASTE OF THE *WHIP.*

ORION IS *NO MAN'S SLAVE!* I SHALL FREE *MYSELF,* AND FORCE MY *SHACKLES* DOWN YOUR--

KZAAAKT

A *PROUD* GROUP, THIS, ADAMSTRANGE. EAGER FOR *LIBERTY,* THEY SEEM.

THEN USE YOUR *MENTAL POWERS.* MONITOR THEIR *THOUGHTS.* IF THEY EVEN *BEGIN* TO PLAN AN *ESCAPE*--

142

EXCELLENT.

THEY THINK DADDY'S *CRAZY*, ALEEA! YEEESS, THEY *DO!* YEEESS, THEY *DO!*

BUT DADDY KNOWS MOMMY'S COMING *HOME!* WON'T THAT BE *EXCITING?*

MOMMEE?

WE LEAVE YOU TO YOUR *BLUEPRINTS*, ADAMSTRANGE, ARCANE AS THEY *ARE* TO US.

THE ONE CALLED *SUPERMAN* HAS ALREADY RESEEDED THE *XYBB* FOREST. HE REQUIRES... *OBSERVATION.*

ATTENTION! INCOMING TRANSMISSION!

ADAM! WHAT'S YOUR *PROGRESS?*

EVERY-THING IS PROCEEDING AS *PLANNED* ... AND AS *ENVI-SIONED.*

BEFORE LONG, RANN WILL BE FULLY PREPARED FOR YOUR *ARRIVAL.*

DO HURRY.

THREE MORE DEGREES TO THE *LEFT*... *TWO* MORE... PERFECT!

WHAT'S THAT *PINGING* NOISE?

ORION'S *MOTHER BOX.* IT HELPS CONTROL HIS *RAGE*... AND IT'S WORKING *OVERTIME.*

BARDA'S *EXPLAINED* TO HIM THAT WE HAVE TO BE *PATIENT*...

...BUT SHE AND ORION ARE *GODS*, AND *ENSLAVEMENT* ISN'T SITTING WELL WITH *EITHER* OF THEM.

PING PING PING PING

NOW, ON TO THE *SOLAR GARDENS*...

POWERSPHERE GOES *HERE,* SAYS THE MAN. YOU *GOT* IT?

WAIT... I'M LOSING MY *GRIP*...

...CAN'T *HOLD* IT...!

THOOM!

... WHAT HAVE YOU *DONE?*

I WISH MY **HUSBAND** WERE HERE. HE'D HAVE US FREED BY NOW.

ADAM HAS TURNED RANN INTO A PRISON TO RIVAL **TAKRON-GALTOS.**

SOME ⸘NNNH⸘ SOME **ALLY.** FOR THE LAST TIME...

...WHO **IS** THIS LUNATIC?

A SOUL RAVAGED BY **GRIEF.**

"ADAM WAS ONCE AN **EARTH ARCHAEOLOGIST** WHO, BY ACCIDENT, ENCOUNTERED THE **ZETA-BEAM**--

"--A TELEPORTATION RAY WHICH TRANS-PORTED HIM 25 TRILLION MILES TO THE FUTURISTIC PLANET RANN.

"THOUGH THE **EFFECTS OF THE RAY** WERE ONLY **TEMPORARY,** ADAM OFTEN RODE SUBSEQUENT **ZETA-BEAMS** TO RANN--

"--BECOMING ITS **CHAMPION,** DEMONSTRATING **COURAGE** AND **CLEVERNESS UNMATCHED**--

"--AND, IN TIME, MARRYING RANN'S **PRINCESS,** THE BEAUTIFUL **ALANNA.**

"EVENTUALLY, ALANNA'S FATHER, **SARDATH,** FOUND A WAY TO MAKE ADAM A **PERMANENT RESIDENT OF RANN**--

"--ONLY TO HAVE HIM STAND BY **HELPLESSLY** AS ALANNA **DIED** GIVING BIRTH TO THEIR DAUGHTER, **ALEEA.**

"SO STRONG WAS ADAM'S **LOVE** FOR HIS BRIDE, IT WAS THE STUFF OF **GALACTIC LEGEND.** HIS LOSS WAS AKIN TO THE **DYING OF A SUN,** SO COLD DID IT LEAVE HIS HEART."

FINE. LET'S START WITH *YOU.*

WRAMM

I AM QUEEN OF THE *AMAZONS.* WE ARE NO *STRANGERS* TO SLAVERY.

BUT WHEN HELD CAPTIVE, WE DID NOT *SEETHE.* INSTEAD, WE *STUDIED* OUR CAPTORS... AND DEVELOPED *STRATEGIES* TO DEFEAT THEM.

YOU ARE NO FOOL, ORION. WHEN YOUR HEAD IS *COOL,* YOU ARE, LIKE ME, A *TACTICIAN.* YOU FIND YOUR ENEMY'S *VULNERABILITIES...* AND STRIKE *THEN.*

EVEN THE *DOG OF WAR* KNOWS WHEN *BEST* TO *BITE.*

SPOKEN LIKE A *WARRIOR BORN*. VERY WELL. I WILL STAY MY HAND... FOR *NOW*.

THANK YOU, ORION.

AMAZING. YOU HAVE *TAMED* HIM... THOUGH I FEAR IT WILL NOTT

LLAAASSTT FFOORR

LLLOOONNNGGG

IT MAY NOT *HAVE* TO WONDER WOMAN, I'M LENDING YOU MY *SPEED*. IT'S OUR ONLY CHANCE.

THE *GUARDS* MONITOR OUR *THOUGHTS*-- BUT THE FOUR OF *US* MOVE *FASTER* THAN THOUGHT!

WE HAVE EXACTLY *ONE SECOND* TO COME UP WITH A *PLAN* BEFORE THE *EN'TARANS RETALIATE*.

SO... WHO'S *GOT* SOMETHING?

LET'S MAKE IT *SIMPLE.* ADAM IS *ALONE* AND *UNGUARDED* IN HIS *TOWER.*

WE *RUSH* HIM--

--AND USE THE *MAGIC LASSO* TO *FORCE* HIM TO *TELL* US HOW TO *RELEASE* OUR *SHACKLES.*

SOUNDS LIKE A *WINNER!* HIGH GEAR, EVERYBODY!

THOOM!

GAME'S OVER, ADAM! WE'VE HAD ENOUGH!

WE DEMAND ANSWERS--AND WE WILL HAVE THEM!

YOUR EN'TARAN ENFORCERS CAN'T GET HERE IN TIME TO STOP US FROM SHAKING YOU LIKE A BABY'S RATTLE!

OH, BUT THEY CAN--

KZAAAKK!

--WITH A LITTLE HELP.

WELL DONE, J'ONN. THANK YOU FOR BRINGING THEM.

GOOD TO KNOW THERE'S SOMEONE SENSIBLE ON THE TEAM.

APPARENTLY, I ALONE BELIEVE IN YOUR CAUSE, ADAM. CONSIDER ME FULLY IN YOUR SERVICE.

THEN TAKE THEM BACK TO HOLDING. MAKE AN EXAMPLE OF THEM TOMORROW, WE GO TO DOUBLE SHIFTS.

ATTENTION! INCOMING TRANSMISSION!

ADAM, WE'RE NEARING RANNSPACE! IS EVERYTHING COMING ALONG?

SMOOTHLY.

BY THE TIME YOU ARRIVE, EVERYTHING WILL BE PRECISELY IN PLACE...

...AND, MY DARLING ALANNA, RANN WILL BE OUR PARADISE ONCE MORE...!

TO BE CONCLUDED!

FOUR DAYS AGO, THE *JUSTICE LEAGUERS* FOUND THEMSELVES TRANSPORTED TO THE DISTANT PLANET *RANN* IN THE *ALPHA CENTAURI* SYSTEM.

SINCE THAT TIME, THEY HAVE BEEN WORKING *AROUND THE CLOCK...*

...RESTORING *BEAUTY* AND *GRANDEUR* TO A WORLD DEVASTATED IN YEARS PAST BY *WAR* AND *NATURAL DISASTER.*

IT WOULD BE A MISSION OF *MERCY* BUT FOR *ONE* THING.

THEY'RE NOT GOING ABOUT IT *WILLINGLY.*

THE LEAGUERS, ALONG WITH EVERYONE *ELSE* ON THE PLANET RANN, ARE OVERSEEN ...AND *PUNISHED*...BY THE TELEPATHIC *EN'TARANS.*

THEY ARE NOT *HEROES,* BUT *SLAVES...*

THEY HAVE SOME WEIRD *BOND.* SOMETHING ABOUT BOTH OF THEM HAVING LOST THEIR *FAMILIES.* GIVEN THE *CIRCUM-STANCES,* MY COMPASSION'S A LITTLE *SHALLOW.*

DON'T EVEN *THINK* OF ESCAPING, STEEL. ADAM'S *TELEPATHIC* SLAVEMASTERS WILL *KNOW*--AND *PUNISH* YOU.

THE FLASH IS STILL PAYING FOR HELPING THE OTHERS TRY TO ESCAPE BY LENDING THEM HIS SPEED.*

THIS PRISON IS WORSE THAN THE PLANET *TAKRON-GALTOS.*

*LAST ISSUE. --DAN

PLUS, *ADAM'S* GONE *CRAZY. HE* THINKS HIS WIFE'S COMING BACK FROM THE *DEAD.* ISN'T THAT WHY HE'S GOT US *WORKING* THIS HARD?

TO *REBUILD* RANN--*EXACTLY*--FOR *HER?* GOD, GET ME *OUT* OF HERE...!

PING PING PING

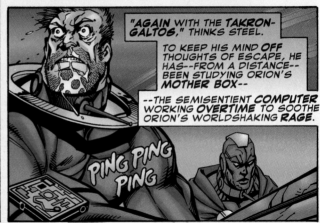

"AGAIN WITH THE *TAKRON-GALTOS,*" THINKS STEEL.

TO KEEP HIS MIND *OFF* THOUGHTS OF ESCAPE, HE HAS--FROM A DISTANCE--BEEN STUDYING ORION'S *MOTHER BOX*--

--THE SEMISENTIENT *COMPUTER* WORKING *OVERTIME* TO SOOTHE ORION'S WORLDSHAKING *RAGE.*

PING PING PING

SO ADEPT AT ANALYZING TECHNOLOGY IS STEEL THAT HE'S GROWN TO IMAGINE A *KINSHIP* WITH THE MOTHER BOX--

--A VAGUE *UNDER-STANDING* OF HOW IT *REGULATES* ORION'S *MOODS*--HOW IT--

PING PING PING PING

--MANIPULATES--

--HIS--

--MIND--

160

...WITH THE RIGHT *ADJUSTMENTS*, IT MIGHT SERVE AS A *TELEPATHIC SHIELD!*

PING PING PING

IN FACT, IF I'M *READING* IT RIGHT, IT'S ACTUALLY *WANTED* TO...BUT UNTIL NOW, IT'S BEEN EXPENDING ALL ITS ENERGY ON CALMING *ORION!*

ORION WON'T *LAST* WITHOUT IT--BUT IF I CAN PLAY THIS *RIGHT*--

--HE WON'T *HAVE* TO--!

--SEE CONSTRUCTION IS NEARLY *FINISHED*, J'ONN--AND NOT A MOMENT TOO *SOON!*

MY BELOVED *ALANNA* IS SCHEDULED TO ARRIVE WITHIN THE *HOUR*--AND, *WITH* HER--

THE *SLAVECOLLAR CONTROLS!* BUT *WHO*--?

!

SKSH.!

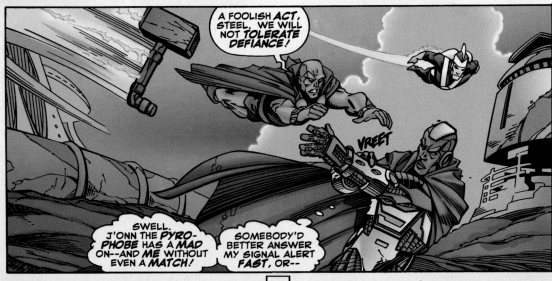

A FOOLISH *ACT*, STEEL. WE WILL NOT *TOLERATE DEFIANCE!*

VREET

SWELL. J'ONN THE *PYRO-PHOBE* HAS A *MAD* ON--AND *ME* WITHOUT EVEN A *MATCH!*

SOMEBODY'D BETTER ANSWER MY SIGNAL ALERT *FAST*, OR--

YEAARGH!!

FWOOSH

BACK OFF, J'ONN!

NICE WORK, STEEL! WITH THESE SLAVE SHACKLES NEUTRALIZED--

--THE EN'TARANS ARE LESS OF A THREAT!

ORION, YOU GUARD ADAM--BUT DON'T HURT HIM. ONCE THIS IS OVER WITH, WE HAVE TO GET HIM SOME HELP.

SUPERMAN, NO! WHAT HAVE YOU DONE?

YOU BROKE LOOSE TOO **SOON!** THE CONSTRUCTION'S NOT **COMPLETE!** MY **GOD,** WE'RE AT THEIR **MERCY--!**

LET IT **REST,** ADAM. WE HAVE A **WORLD** TO LIBERATE. NOW THAT WE'RE **FREE,** WE CAN **HANDLE** A FEW DOZEN **EN'TARANS.**

A FEW **DOZEN?**

HOW ABOUT A FEW **THOUSAND?**

WHAT? BUT...?

IT'S THE **TRUTH,** SUPERMAN.

YOUR UNEXPECTED **REBELLION** HAS PUT THE PLANET **RANN** IN DEADLY DANGER.

J'ONN! STAY **BACK--!**

PLEASE. I AM ON **YOUR** SIDE. I **HAVE** BEEN SINCE THE **START**--AND SO HAS **ADAM.**

YOUR PLAN'S BEEN **THWARTED,** ADAM. YOU MAY AS WELL TELL THEM **EVERY-THING.**

WHY NOT? WE'VE GOT NOTHING TO **LOSE.** IN ABOUT **TWENTY MINUTES,** AN EN'TARAN **INVASION** FLEET IS GOING TO BREAK INTO ORBIT AROUND **RANN**--

--AND **VAPORIZE** THE **PLANET!**

"IT STARTED WITH MY FATHER-IN-LAW, SARDATH. I'D BEEN TOLD ALANNA *DIED* GIVING BIRTH TO OUR DAUGHTER, *ALEEA*--"

"--BUT THAT PRONOUNCEMENT CAME FROM A VISITING *EARTH* DOCTOR *UNFAMILIAR* WITH RANNIAN PHYSIOLOGY.

"UNBEKNOWNST TO ME, SARDATH--ALMOST AS OVER-COME WITH GRIEF AS *I*--FOUND AN EMBER OF LIFE STILL *SMOLDERING* WITHIN ALANNA AND SECRETLY STOLE *AWAY* WITH HER *PRESERVED* BODY.

"CLINGING TO THE *SLIMMEST* OF HOPES, SARDATH SPENT THE NEXT COUPLE OF YEARS TRAVELING THE *COSMOS*, IN SEARCH OF ANYONE WHO MIGHT BE ABLE TO *REVIVE* HER.

"DESPERATE, HE FINALLY SURRENDERED ALANNA TO THE *EN'TARANS*, A RACE OF TELEPATHIC *CONQUERORS*, WHO *INDEED* BROUGHT HER BACK TO *LIFE*--BUT AT A COST SARDATH DID NOT *FORESEE*.

"BECAUSE ALANNA, *TOO*, ONCE USED THE ZETA-BEAM THAT BROUGHT ME TO RANN FROM EARTH, THE EN'TARANS UNLOCKED A TRACE OF *ZETA RADIATION* IN HER *CELLS*--

"--AND, REALIZING ITS *CAPABILITY*, ENVISIONED USING ITS *TELEPORTATION* PROPERTIES TO CONQUER THE *GALAXY*.

"I KNEW NONE OF THIS--YET--WHEN I RECEIVED THE MOST SHOCKING MESSAGE OF MY *LIFE*..."

'SOKAY, SWEETIE. FUNNY HEADBAND'S CALLED A *MENTICIZER*. IT'LL HELP TEACH YOU TO *TALK*...

HEA'BAND?

ATTENTION! INCOMING TRANSMISSION!

ADAM! ADAM, CAN YOU *HEAR* ME?

ALANNA? IS IT...REALLY *YOU*?

YOU... YOU'RE... *ALIVE*...? HOW-- WHERE--?

MY LOVE, I'M... *STRANDED!* BRING ME HOME--AND HURRY! SET A ZETA-BEAM FOR THE *FOLLOWING* COORDINATES...

"I DID AS SHE ASKED--BUT SUSPICION GOT THE BETTER OF ME. CONSULTING A *STARCHART*, I MATCHED THE COORDINATES TO THE *EN'TARAN HOMEWORLD*--

"--AND, ON A *HUNCH*, ADAPTED THE MENTICIZER TO GUARD AGAINST TELEPATHIC *SCANS* SHOULD THIS BE AN EN'TARAN *TRICK*--

"--WHICH, OF COURSE, IT *WAS*. *THEY* ARRIVED, *NOT* ALANNA--AND IN AS GREAT A NUMBER AS THE ZETA-BEAM WOULD *ALLOW*."

HOLDING ALANNA AND SARDATH *HOSTAGE*, THEY DEMANDED I SURRENDER THE ZETA TECHNOLOGY--

--AND, FEARING TRICKERY THEM-*SELVES*, SENT AN ENTIRE *FLEET* TO *RETRIEVE* IT.

IN CASE THEY MET WITH *RESISTANCE*, THEY WERE PREPARED TO *INCINERATE* US.

WE STILL HAVE **ONE CHANCE** FOR MY PLAN TO **WORK**.

WHAT **PLAN?** I STILL DON'T UNDERSTAND WHY ALL THIS **CONSTRUCTION** WAS--

TRICKED US, YOU DID, ADAMSTRANGE!

ALANNA AND SARDATH, **DEAD** THEY ARE!

HSSS!

HSSS!

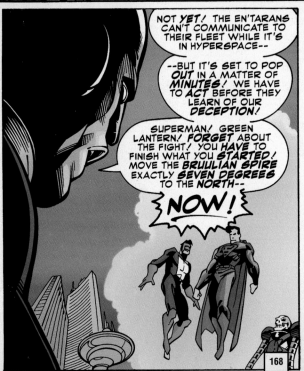

NOT **YET!** THE EN'TARANS CAN'T COMMUNICATE TO THEIR FLEET WHILE IT'S IN HYPERSPACE--

--BUT IT'S SET TO POP **OUT** IN A MATTER OF **MINUTES!** WE HAVE TO **ACT** BEFORE THEY LEARN OF OUR **DECEPTION!**

SUPERMAN! GREEN LANTERN! **FORGET** ABOUT THE FIGHT! YOU **HAVE** TO FINISH WHAT YOU **STARTED!** MOVE THE **BRUULIAN SPIRE** EXACTLY **SEVEN DEGREES** TO THE **NORTH**--

NOW!

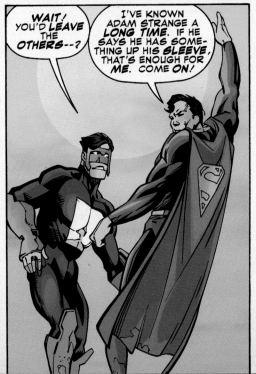

WAIT! YOU'D **LEAVE** THE **OTHERS**--?

I'VE KNOWN ADAM STRANGE A **LONG TIME.** IF HE SAYS HE HAS SOMETHING UP HIS **SLEEVE,** THAT'S ENOUGH FOR **ME.** COME **ON!**

I WAS **NEVER RE-CONSTRUCTING** RANN--NOT **EXACTLY.** THAT WAS ALL **CAMOUFLAGE.**

"INSTEAD I WAS HIDING IN **PLAIN SIGHT** CERTAIN **KEY STRUCTURES** LACED WITH **CIRCUITRY** AND **TRANSFORMERS.**

"THEY HAD TO BE LAID WITH **MACHINE PRECISION** WHILE APPEARING TOTALLY **INNOCENT.**

"NO LAB-CREATED ZETA BEAM COULD HOPE TO BANISH THE VAST **EN'TARAN FLEET**--BUT IF WE DID THE **JOB** RIGHT--"

--THE **ENTIRE PLANET** RANN IS NOW ONE GIANT ZETA BEAM PROJECTOR--

--AND **I'M ITS LENS!**

YOU--?

ZETA TELEPORTATION IS **TEMPORARY.** I STAY ON RANN ONLY BECAUSE **MY BODY** CONTAINS **MEGA-ZETA** RADIATION--THE ONLY **LASTING** ZETA THERE IS.

ONCE THE BEAM FIRES **THROUGH** ME, IT WILL DRAW THAT RADIA-TION **OUT**--AND TELEPORT THE EN'TARANS AWAY **PERMANENTLY!**

THE BEAM'S ALMOST *READY.* SUPERMAN, *SARDATH* AND *ALANNA* ARE DEPENDING ON *YOU.* YOU'VE GOT TO GET THEM *FREE* BEFORE THE BEAM *STRIKES!*

BY *OUTRACING* IT? I'M NOT FASTER THAN *LIGHT*--!

I CAN--

FLASH CAN LEND SPEED! POOL YOUR POWER!

BRACE YOURSELF, SUPES--I'M NOT HOLDING BACK!

YOU WERE COUNTING ON *ALL THIS COMING TOGETHER?* WASN'T THAT ONE HELL OF A *GAMBLE?*

IF I'D CONTACTED THE *SEVEN SOLDIERS OF VICTORY* IT WOULD BE A *GAMBLE.*

I BROUGHT THE *JUSTICE LEAGUE.*

THAT'S A *PLAN.*

"ADAM, *WAIT!* WON'T THE ZETA-BEAM DRAW THE EN'TARANS *PLANETSIDE?*"

"I'VE BUILT A *RELAY* INTO THE *TRANSMITTER* TO *REROUTE RECEPTION*-- SEND THEM SOMEWHERE *ELSE.* GET *SET*--"

"YOU'VE *GOT* TO OUTRACE THAT BEAM, SUPERMAN--"

SSKOW

NOW!

IT WORKED! IT WORKED!

WHERE'D YOU SEND THEM?

BARDA WILL APPRECIATE THIS.

"I BEAMED THEM TO TAKRON-GALTOS."

SUPERMAN, HURRY....!

EASY, ADAM. YOU DON'T WANT ALANNA TO BURN UP IN RE-ENTRY. I KNOW YOU'RE ANXIOUS TO SEE HER... BUT WE WON, MAN! RELAX!

YOU'VE GOT ALL THE TIME IN THE...

...OH. OH, GOD.

I JUST REALIZED! YOU DREW THE MEGA-ZETA RADIATION OUT OF YOURSELF! WITH IT GONE--

THERE YOU ARE!

WE'VE BEEN SEARCHING THE *GALAXY* FOR YOU EIGHT!

EIGHT? WHERE'S ADAM?

REMEMBER, THE ZETA BEAM RETURNS YOU TO YOUR POINT OF *ORIGIN.* ADAM'S BACK ON EARTH SOMEWHERE...

...ALONE.

WOW. ONE GUY AGAINST AN ENTIRE *RACE* OF *INVADERS*... AND HE BEAT THEM BY *OUTTHINKING* THEM.

AND I THOUGHT *BATMAN* WAS GOOD.

SOME *REWARD,* THOUGH...RIPPED AWAY FROM HIS *WIFE* AND *KID.* RIGHT, J'ONN?

J'ONN...?

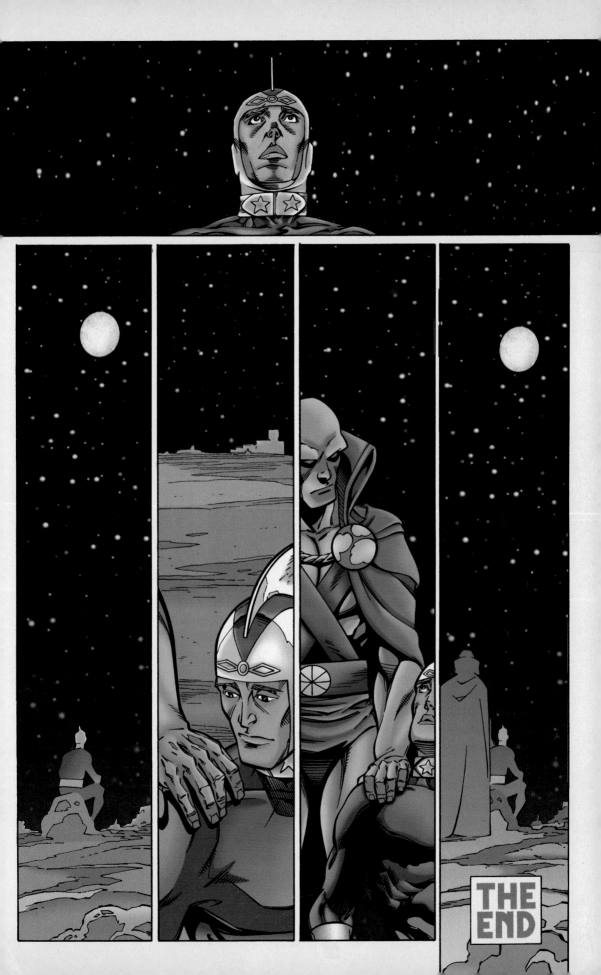

THE END

RETURN OF THE
CONQUEROR

MICHAEL HANEY'S GOT SOMETHING ON HIS MIND. HE EVEN FORGOT THE WORDS OF THE OATH IN CLASS TODAY... "I PLEDGE ALLEGIANCE TO THE CONQUEROR..." AND SAID SOMETHING DIFFERENT.

IT'S NOT JUST BECAUSE HE GOT IN TROUBLE: HE KNOWS SOMETHING'S NOT RIGHT WITH THE WORLD.

HE KNOWS SOMETHING'S MISSING.

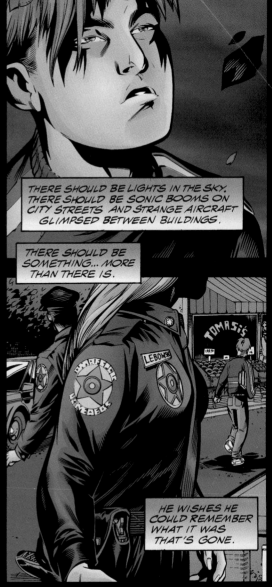

THERE SHOULD BE LIGHTS IN THE SKY. THERE SHOULD BE SONIC BOOMS ON CITY STREETS AND STRANGE AIRCRAFT GLIMPSED BETWEEN BUILDINGS.

THERE SHOULD BE SOMETHING... MORE THAN THERE IS.

HE WISHES HE COULD REMEMBER WHAT IT WAS THAT'S GONE.

AND IT WATCHES.

IT KNOWS.

SOMETHING IS MISSING.

SOMETHING IS WRONG AND ONLY MICHAEL SEEMS TO CARE.

AND SO, IN HIS ROOM, ON ANOTHER HOT SUMMER NIGHT, MICHAEL HANEY LIES DOWN ONE MORE TIME WITH HIS PAPER AND HIS PENS AND TRIES TO IMAGINE WHAT THAT SOMETHING COULD BE...

HE TRIES HIS BEST TO GIVE IT A SHAPE.

HE TRIES TO GIVE IT A NAME.

AND IT TRIES TO STOP HIM.

GRANT MORRISON
WRITER
JOHN DELL
INKER
PAT GARRAHY
COLORIST
L.A. WILLIAMS
ASSISTANT EDITOR

HOWARD PORTER
PENCILLER
KENNY LOPEZ
LETTERER
HEROIC AGE
SEPARATOR
DAN RASPLER
EDITOR

JLA Roll Call

Superman   Wonder   Zauriel   Martian   Green   Aquaman   Flash   Batman
            Woman   Manhunter Lantern

METROPOLIS

LOIS?

LOIS?

LOIS.
MY GOD.

JLA PRIORITY TELEPATHIC ALARM!

THIS IS SUPERMAN.

WE'VE GOT A PROBLEM.

ORACLE? J'ONN?

IS ANYONE THERE?

SUPERMAN. GLAD YOU'VE JOINED US.

J'ONN, IS THAT YOU? WHAT'S BEEN HAPPENING?

THE WHOLE OF METROPOLIS IS ASLEEP. EVEN I ALMOST DIDN'T WAKE UP...

GOTHAM, STAR CITY, TORONTO, MIAMI...NO ONE IS WAKING UP!

MY GOD.

PEOPLE ARE FALLING ASLEEP WHERE THEY STAND!

THE NEAREST FULLY ALERT DELTA BRAINWAVE I'M PICKING UP ON IS IN PANAMA IN THE SOUTH, AND...

PLEASE COME IN. WHO ELSE IS AWAKE AND ON DUTY?

I DON'T KNOW. I'M ALWAYS AWAKE, SUPERMAN.

SUPERMAN. THIS IS ZAURIEL ON TELEPATHIC LINK. WHERE ARE YOU?

ARCTIC CIRCLE. I'LL BE RIGHT WITH YOU.

STEEL, PLASTIC MAN. HUNTRESS, ORACLE...ALL SLEEPING. SO WHY ARE WE STILL AWAKE?

I WAS A GUARDIAN ANGEL; I HAVEN'T SLEPT SINCE THE DAWN OF CREATION.

I DIDN'T WANT TO MISS ANY MORE DAWNS THAT GOOD.

TOO BAD ABOUT THIS ONE.

HI. WELCOME TO THE AERIE.

IT HAPPENED AT 3:30, SAME TIME THE STORMS BEGAN TO BUILD. I'VE DONE WHAT I CAN HERE.

FLASH AND BATMAN ARE BOTH AWAKE, THERE'S BEEN NO WORD SO FAR FROM AQUAMAN, AND THE OTHERS ARE ON THE MOON.

AND THERE'S SOMETHING ELSE...

SANDMAN, WHOEVER YOU ARE, WHEREVER YOU CAME FROM...RIGHT NOW WE NEED ANSWERS.

WHAT DO YOU KNOW ABOUT WHAT'S HAPPENING?

It is much older than you can imagine.

It has been stalking this world and now, like a tiger, it strikes. It conquers first in dreams, then in reality.

IT? OUR LOVED ONES ARE UNDER THREAT, SANDMAN!

IT SOUNDS LIKE SOME KIND OF ALIEN, SUPERMAN. WE DON'T REALLY KNOW WHAT IT IS OR WHAT IT DOES...

YOU'RE ONE OF THEM, AREN'T YOU? THE ENDLESS...

Dream cannot die, nor am I Morpheus.

You're far from the Silver City, angel.

All who sleep here dream ITS dream.

They will become first Its slaves and finally Its nourishment. And the feast will attract others. Divisions of It.

Your people will die in chains. It will exhaust your worlds resources and pass on. You will have become It.

IN HEAVEN, THERE WERE WHISPERS OF THE IMMANENT ONES BUT... DIDN'T I HEAR THAT MORPHEUS, THE DREAM KING, WAS DEAD?

I PREFER THE POLLUTION AND THE NOISE HERE.

DO YOU KNOW WHY EVERYONE'S ASLEEP?

I heard a child calling from the depths of the dream in which he drowns. He was calling you.

I took pity on him and I come here to bring you his petition.

IF YOU ARE WHO YOU CLAIM TO BE, SANDMAN, YOU MUST HAVE THE POWER TO PROTECT THE DREAM KINGDOM FROM ANY THREAT.

Must I?

This is about a child's faith, not about the extent of my sovereignty.

He clings to the belief that you will come to his rescue, even though he can barely remember what you are.

If you do not, he will wake in Its power, like everyone else. They will be It. You will succumb, in the end, to It.

189

GOTHAM CITY:

IT HAPPENED AT 6:30 EASTERN TIME. I WAS ON MY WAY HOME TO BED.

PEOPLE IN THE HOSPITALS ARE GOING TO BE OUR FIRST PROBLEM.

THAT'S BEFORE WE EVEN START THINKING ABOUT WORLDWIDE ECONOMIC COLLAPSE...

SOMETHING THAT CAN'T HAVE ESCAPED YOUR NOTICE, J'ONN:

BLUE VALLEY, IN ADDITION TO BEING WHERE THE FLASH GREW UP, IS ALSO WHERE WE CONFRONTED THAT ALIEN PARASITE LAST YEAR...

THE CONNECTION HAD OCCURRED TO ME, BATMAN.

BUT THIS SLEEP PLAGUE IS UNLIKE ANYTHING WE ENCOUNTERED THEN.

SO FAR, I HAVE A REQUEST.

I NEED SOMETHING FROM THE WATCHTOWER TROPHY ROOM...

MAYDAY! REPEAT! IS THERE ANYONE ON THE GROUND? MAYDAY!

I'LL PASS IT ALONG.

EXCUSE ME, BATMAN. I MAY BE A LITTLE PREOCCUPIED FOR THE NEXT FEW MINUTES...

191

THIS IS ZAURIEL ON THE WATCHTOWER.

I'M ON MY WAY TO THE TROPHY ROOM NOW, J'ONN. I'M ALERTING ALL INBOUND AIRCRAFT.

LIKE A DIAMOND TURNED INSIDE OUT FOREVER REFLECTING THE INFINITE GLORY OF THE PRESENCE A HYMN WITHOUT BEGINNING OR END

I'M GOING TO ATTEMPT A SUBORBITAL RECONNAISSANCE OF THE CONTINENT, IN CASE WE MISSED SOMETHING.

ZAURIEL?

WHAT WAS THAT I EXPERIENCED?

J'ONN, SORRY. IT WAS MY OVER-MIND. MY ANGEL-MIND.

ALL THE EXCITEMENT, IT JUST LEAKED IN. SORRY IF I STARTLED YOU.

OKAY, I HAVE IT HERE.

WHY DOES BATMAN NEED THIS?

IT WAS THE FIRST THING I THOUGHT OF.

I MEAN, LET'S FACE IT, I WAS THE GUY WHO GOT TAKEN OVER BY ONE OF THOSE THINGS LAST TIME.

BUT IT WAS OBVIOUS WHEN I SAW BLUE VALLEY.

THE ONLY PEOPLE AWAKE IN THE WHOLE OF NORTH AMERICA WERE IN DIRECT CONTACT WITH THESE...AH... THESE FACE-HUGGER THINGS.

APART FROM WONDER WOMAN, WHO WAS ON THE MOON, AND ZAURIEL, WHO NEVER SLEEPS AT ALL, APPARENTLY.

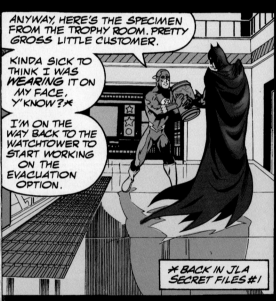

ANYWAY, HERE'S THE SPECIMEN FROM THE TROPHY ROOM. PRETTY GROSS LITTLE CUSTOMER.

KINDA SICK TO THINK I WAS WEARING IT ON MY FACE, Y'KNOW?*

I'M ON THE WAY BACK TO THE WATCHTOWER TO START WORKING ON THE EVACUATION OPTION.

*BACK IN JLA SECRET FILES #1

IS EVERYTHING OKAY? I MEAN, I'M NOT STEPPING ON YOUR TOES, AM I? I MEAN, YOU'RE THE DETECTIVE.

I JUST FIGURED--

WE'RE ALL ADULTS HERE, MR. WEST.

AND RIGHT NOW WE HAVE BIGGER FISH TO FRY.

OKAY. ONE HOUR.

THE DREAMING.

THIS IS IT? STRANGE...

IT REMINDS ME OF MY HOMETOWN.

AND I OF THE MEADOWS OF THEMISCYRA WHEN I WAS YOUNG...

THIS FEELS WEIRD.

AM I DREAMING THIS?

WISHING RING?

I NEVER THOUGHT ABOUT IT LIKE THAT.

THERE'S SOMETHING HERE... I CAN SMELL IT, LIKE SOMETHING FROM THE OCEAN. IT'S LEFT ITS TRACES EVERYWHERE.

of course. This is my country: the Kingdom of Dreams, the land where stories grow and are born into the world.

Your wishing ring may prove the most effective weapon here, Green Lantern.

SANDMAN, WE'RE INSIDE A DREAM THIS CREATURE HAS CONSTRUCTED AS A PRISON CAMP FOR HUMANITY.

WHAT KIND OF RULES CAN WE POSSIBLY EXPECT TO APPLY HERE?

Did you come with a rulebook into the waking world, Superman? You have been here before many times.

SUPERMAN?

Why does he overshadow all of your thoughts and actions?

THAT'S WHAT WORRIES ME.

OKAY, SO WHERE ARE THE BAD GUYS AND WHAT DO WE DO?

Why do you hesitate each time? This man Jordan, the one who wore the magic ring before you...

WHAT? WHAT DOES THIS HAVE TO DO WITH ANYTHING? I WAS JUST THINKING ABOUT... WHAT IS THIS ABOUT, HAL?

You will surpass him. You already know what he could never learn.

SH'YEAH! HAL JORDAN WAS THE BEST. EVERY-BODY KNOWS THAT. EVERYBODY KEEPS TELLING ME THAT, NO MATTER WHAT I DO... I MET HIM; THE GUY WAS A STAR. WHAT COULD I POSSIBLY KNOW THAT HE DIDN'T KNOW?

Fear. You will surpass him.

MICHAEL HANEY HAS A NAME ON THE TIP OF HIS TONGUE. EVERY TIME HE LOOKS AT HIS DRAWING, THE NAME FLOATS UP SO CLOSE TO THE SURFACE HE CAN ALMOST TASTE IT.

IT KNOWS.

IT KNOWS EVERYTHING.

IT SEES EVERYTHING.

IT is not absolute ruler of this country, Michael.

SOMETHING LIKE A GHOST IS STANDING IN MICHAEL HANEY'S ROOM.

AND IT'S TELLING HIM SOMETHING HE'S KNOWN ALL HIS LIFE.

Believe and you will be saved.

BUT IT'S JUST HIS IMAGINATION.

EVERYBODY ALWAYS SAYS HE HAS TOO VIVID AN IMAGINATION.

EVERYBODY KNOWS HE'S A WEIRD KID.

IT KNOWS.

MIKEY...

AND DAD'S VOICE SOUNDS FUNNY AND THICK, LIKE HE'S TALKING THROUGH JELLO.

LIKE IT'S TWO VOICES AT THE SAME TIME.

OR MAYBE IT'S JUST HIS IMAGINATION.

I BROUGHT YOU SOMETHING FROM THE PET STORE.

WEIRD LITTLE CRITTER, AIN'T HE?

NOBODY'S COMING, MICHAEL.

THERE'S NOBODY HERE BUT *IT*.

FOREVER AND EVER.

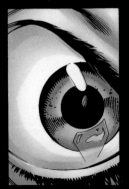

SUPERMAN.

TWO HUNDRED AND FIFTY MILES SOUTH-WEST.

...NO, IT'S GONE, NOW.

JUST LIKE MY STRENGTH. I TOLD YOU.

WE'RE IN *IT'S* DREAM, SUPERMAN. *IT'S* MORE POWERFUL HERE THAN *WE* ARE!

GUYS. DO WE HAVE A PROBLEM?

THERE!

EVEN MY SUPER-SIGHT IS FAILING BUT I... GREAT SCOTT.

SUPERMAN? WHAT DID YOU SEE?

WE HAVE NO POWERS, THERE ARE MILLIONS OF THEM AND THERE'S A CHILD IN THERE WHO NEEDS US TO SAVE THE WORLD.

LET'S GO.

SUPERMAN AND THE OTHERS HAVE BEEN ASLEEP FOR EIGHTEEN MINUTES. EVERYTHING OKAY, J'ONN?

ZAURIEL! I THOUGHT I FELT SOMETHING MOVE. SOMETHING SO BIG AND SO SLOW...

THERE! ON THE EDGE OF CONSCIOUSNESS.

HEY! CAREFUL UP THERE, J'ONN.

YOU CAN'T BREATHE IN SPACE, CAN YOU? I'M JUST BEING DEN MOTHER...

I CAN HOLD MY BREATH, FLASH.

THE CLOUDS ARE DISPERSING BELOW ME...

AQUAMAN! IS THAT YOU? WHERE ARE YOU?

NOVA SCOTIA. SORRY, I WAS TOO BUSY TO CHECK IN.

I CAUGHT THE END OF THAT, J'ONN. I CAN CONFIRM THAT THERE'S A...PRESENCE IN THE OCEAN. IT'S NORTH OF HERE, I THINK.

IT'S BIG. IT'S CAUSING THE STORMS.

THIS IS THE TAPE FROM THE BLUE VALLEY INCIDENT LAST YEAR, ZAURIEL.

I AM THE PROBE.

HE IS THE CONQUEROR.

I'LL BE RIGHT WITH YOU, FLASH. IT'S JUST...

THERE'S SOMETHING HERE...

I AM THE PROBE.

HE IS THE CONQUEROR.

WHO IS THE CONQUEROR?

IF THAT WAS ONLY... A PROBE... WHAT WAS IT LOOKING FOR AND...

FLASH...

WAIT A MINUTE... WHAT'S THAT?

SEE WHERE THE STORMS ARE BEGINNING TO CLEAR OVER CANADA?

J'ONN, WHAT IS THAT? THERE'S SOMETHING HUGE ON MY SCREEN...

DO YOU HAVE VISUAL CONTACT, J'ONN?

FLASH, I...

FLASH, THERE ARE DOZENS OF THEM, COMING OUT OF NOWHERE... GIGANTIC...

WE'RE BEING INVADED...

I CAN SEE IT.

MOONS OF MARS.

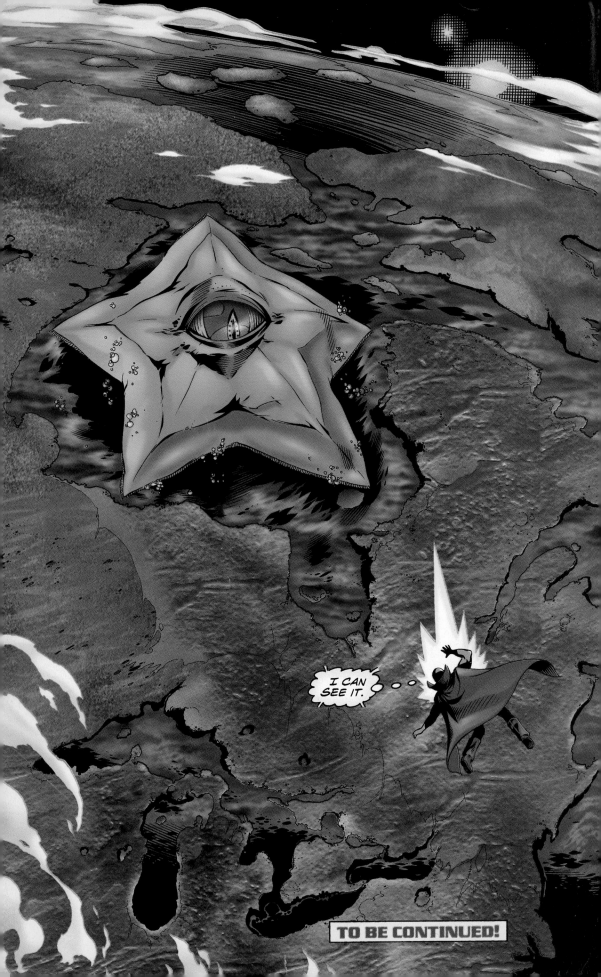

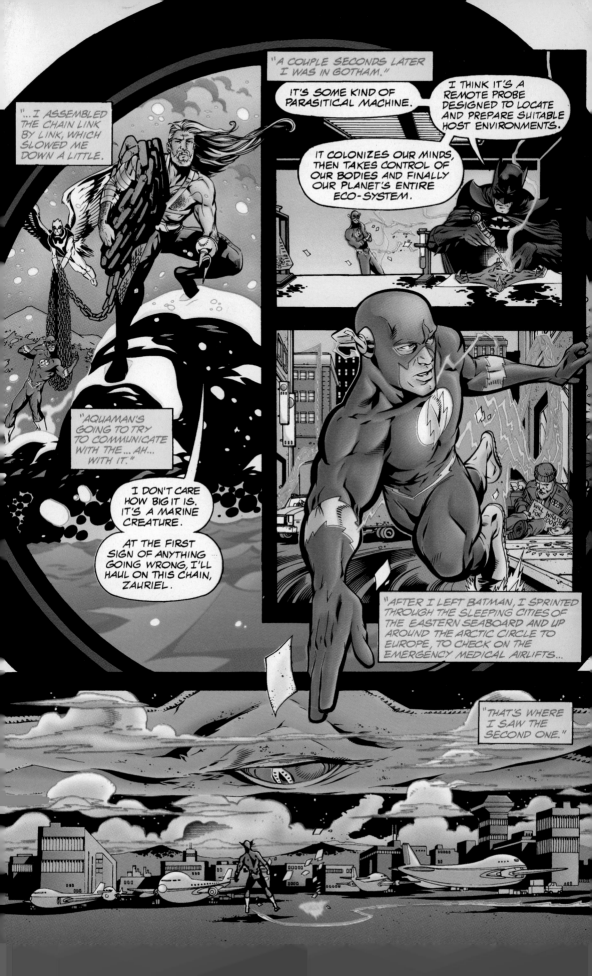

"J'ONN, THESE THINGS ARE FLOATING THERE, WAITING TO LATCH ONTO EVERY CONTINENT ON EARTH.

"BY TOMORROW, IT WON'T JUST BE EVERYONE IN NORTH AMERICA WHO'S AFFECTED...

...THE WHOLE WORLD'S GOING TO BE ASLEEP, UNDER THE CONTROL OF THOSE THINGS.

THEY'RE STILL MAINTAINING A HOLDING PATTERN IN EARTH ORBIT.

THEY SEEM TO BE WAITING FOR A SIGNAL, FLASH. THAT GIVES US TIME.

AND WHAT ABOUT LANTERN AND THE OTHERS? THEY'VE BEEN IN THAT DREAM WORLD OR WHATEVER IT IS FOR ALMOST AN HOUR.

CAN WE TRUST THIS SANDMAN GUY? I MEAN, THE 'GOD OF DREAMS'... COME ON!

HE'S MORE THAN A GOD. ON MARS, LONG AGO, WE KNEW HIM AS LORD L'ZORIL. ONCE I MET HIM HERE, ON EARTH.

BELIEVE ME, WE HAVE NO CHOICE BUT TO TRUST HIM.

IT COMES FIRST IN YOUR DREAMS.

THEN YOUR DREAM BECOMES *ITS* DREAM.

IT DIVIDES. IT INVADES. IT CONQUERS. AND IN THE END, WHEN YOU WAKE AND OPEN YOUR EYES, THERE'S NO MORE YOU

THERE'S ONLY IT.

MICHAEL HANEY KNOWS.

THAT'S WHY IT HAS TO STOP HIM.

HE KNOWS THERE'S SOMETHING STRONGER THAN IT.

IF ONLY HE COULD REMEMBER WHAT THAT THING IS.

THERE MUST BE THOUSANDS... MILLIONS...

I COULD HAVE COUNTED THEM WITH A GLANCE IF WE STILL HAD OUR POWERS, WONDER WOMAN.

LET'S HOPE SANDMAN HAS SOMETHING UP HIS SLEEVE.

SH'YEAH, RIGHT!

WHERE'D HE DISAPPEAR TO?

205

HIGH ON A HILL, THE KING OF STORIES STANDS AND WATCHES.

AND THE DREAM UNFOLDS.

CONQUERORS

GRANT
MORRISON
writer

HOWARD
PORTER
penciller

JOHN
DELL
inker

KENNY LOPEZ
letterer

L.A. WILLIAMS
assistant editor

PAT GARRAHY
colorist

DAN RASPLER
editor

HEROIC AGE
separator

...NOTHING BUT BLACKNESS DOWN THERE. IT'S LIKE INK... I DON'T UNDERSTAND WHY...

I SHOULD BE ABLE TO SEE IT BY--

AQUAMAN?

WHAT WAS THAT?

I'M NOT SURE WHAT I JUST SAW... LOOKED LIKE THE WHOLE SEA BED SHIFTED...WHAT WAS...

...MY GOD...

AQUAMAN! IT'S INFILTRATING YOUR CONSCIOUSNESS!

LET ME WORK THROUGH YOU! I'M EXPERIENCED IN PSYCHO-COMBAT TECHNIQUES.

...OCEANS BEYOND SPACE AND TIME... GRAVITY SEWERS... IT... CRAWLS FREE... IT DIVIDES... IT INVADES...

NO I WILL NOT!

...I RULE THE SEAS!... LAUGHABLE COMPARED TO THIS...IT'S OLDER THAN TIME... I WILL NOT KNEEL...IT...

IT DIVIDES... IT CONQUERS...

OKAY.

THESE ARE FILES ON SIMILAR CREATURES YOU AND THE OLD LEAGUE ENCOUNTERED, J'ONN.

IF BATMAN'S RIGHT, MAYBE THIS WAS THE FIRST PROBE AND MAYBE WE...

BOOM!

UH-OH.

GREEN LANTERN'S DOWN!

WE HAVE TO HELP HIM!

WE HAVE A CHILD TO SAVE, SUPERMAN. ACCORDING TO SANDMAN, HE HOLDS THE KEY TO DEFEATING THIS "IT." HE'S OUR PRIORITY.

I'LL CLEAR A PATH AND HOLD THEM AS LONG AS I CAN.

MICHAEL HANEY ALWAYS KNEW THERE WAS SOMETHING MISSING FROM THE WORLD.

TRAPPED IN ITS DREAM, HE TRIED TO IMAGINE SOMETHING BETTER, SOMETHING STRONGER.

SOMETHING STRONGER THAN IT.

NOT FAR AWAY, GROTESQUE, INHUMAN SHOUTING DIES AWAY.

AND FOR A MOMENT...

ALL SEEMS LOST.

SUH-SUPERMAN?

AND THEN HE REMEMBERS EVERYTHING.

SUPERMAN!

SHH... RRRAKK

WUHH.

FASTER THAN A SPEEDING BULLET...

I'VE GOT YOU, SON.

"AND ORION APPEARS TO HAVE WOUNDED IT."

PAIN... IT'S IN *SHOCK*... DEFENSIVE SYSTEMS...

RETALIATE... IT'S GOING TO...

AQUAMAN!

RRRAAAAA!

I HAVE ORION. HE'S ALIVE.

WHAT HAPPENED?

BATMAN? DO WE HAVE THE SIGNAL YET?

WHERE IS AQUAMAN? ZAURIEL!

NOW!

I HAVE AN ALIEN TRANSMISSION SEQUENCE I NEED TO PASS THROUGH YOUR CONSCIOUSNESS, AQUAMAN.

CALM YOUR MIND, MAINTAIN CONTACT WITH THE CREATURE.

IT KNOWS WE'RE HERE, J'ONN!

IT'S GETTING READY FOR ANOTHER ATTACK.

SO THAT MEANS I CAN MAKE ANYTHING HAPPEN.

WHAT **IS** IT?

A nightmare, nothing more.

IT HAS ENCOUNTERED A HOSTILE ENVIRONMENT.

IT MUST WITHDRAW. ALL DIVISIONS OF IT MUST WITHDRAW.

THE BOY'S SAFE, SANDMAN.

WHAT NOW? HOW DO WE DEFEAT THAT THING?

You've done what I brought you here for.

Go now.

This dream, ITS dream, is over.

NMM.

IT TRIES TO RUN.

IT TRIES TO HIDE.

BUT THE DREAM IS EVERYWHERE.

YAAAA

YOU TOLD ME TO WAKE YOU UP IN AN HOUR.

TIME'S UP.

THAT WAS AN HOUR?

GREAT HERA.

FLASH, WHAT HAPPENED? DID WE DO IT?

WE'RE THE JUSTICE LEAGUE, SUPERMAN.

WHAT DO YOU THINK?

GOOD MORNING, NORTH AMERICA! THIS IS THE FLASH!

THE DREAM FADES.

IT HAS GONE, A MEMORY ON THE FRAYED EDGES OF SLEEP.

ACROSS A CONTINENT, MILLIONS OF EYES OPEN AT ONCE.

MICHAEL HANEY WAKES AND SNIFFS THE AIR AND FEELS THE WEIGHT OF THE REAL WORLD SETTLE ON HIS SHOULDERS.

HE REMEMBERS BEING A LITTLE BOY. HE REMEMBERS BEING CARRIED THROUGH THE AIR, FAR FROM CARE.

HE REMEMBERS SAVING THE WORLD.

BUT THAT'S ALWAYS BEEN THE THING ABOUT MICHAEL.

TOO VIVID AN IMAGINATION.

THE STARS OF THE DC UNIVERSE CAN ALSO BE FOUND IN THESE BOOKS:

GRAPHIC NOVELS

DARKSEID VS. GALACTUS: THE HUNGER
John Byrne

ENEMY ACE: WAR IDYLL
George Pratt

GREEN LANTERN: GANTHET'S TALE
Larry Niven/John Byrne

GREEN LANTERN/SILVER SURFER
Ron Marz/Darryl Banks/Terry Austin

THE POWER OF SHAZAM!
Jerry Ordway

TITANS: SCISSORS, PAPER, STONE
Adam Warren/Tom Simmons/Joe Rosas

COLLECTIONS

AQUAMAN: TIME & TIDE
Peter David/Kirk Jarvinen/Brad Vancata

THE AMALGAM AGE OF COMICS: THE DC COMICS COLLECTION
Various writers and artists

DC VERSUS MARVEL/ MARVEL VERSUS DC
Ron Marz/Peter David/Dan Jurgens/ Claudio Castellini/Josef Rubinstein/ Paul Neary

THE FLASH: THE RETURN OF BARRY ALLEN
Mark Waid/Greg LaRocque/Roy Richardson

THE GOLDEN AGE
James Robinson/Paul Smith/Richard Ory

THE GREATEST 1950S STORIES EVER TOLD
Various writers and artists

THE GREATEST TEAM-UP STORIES EVER TOLD
Various writers and artists

HAWK & DOVE
Karl & Barbara Kesel/Rob Liefeld

HITMAN
Garth Ennis/John McCrea

IMPULSE: RECKLESS YOUTH
Mark Waid/Humberto Ramos/ Wayne Faucher/various

KINGDOM COME
Mark Waid/Alex Ross

LEGENDS: THE COLLECTED EDITION
John Ostrander/Len Wein/John Byrne/ Karl Kesel

LOBO'S GREATEST HITS
Various writers and artists

LOBO: THE LAST CZARNIAN
Keith Giffen/Alan Grant/Simon Bisley

LOBO'S BACK'S BACK
Keith Giffen/Alan Grant/Simon Bisley/ Christian Alamy

RETURN TO THE AMALGAM AGE OF COMICS: THE DC COMICS COLLECTION
Various writers and artists

THE RAY: IN A BLAZE OF POWER
Jack C. Harris/Joe Quesada/Art Nichols

SOVEREIGN SEVEN
Chris Claremont/Dwayne Turner/ Jerome Moore/various

THE SPECTRE: CRIMES AND PUNISHMENTS
John Ostrander/Tom Mandrake

STARMAN: NIGHT AND DAY
James Robinson/Tony Harris/ Wade von Grawbadger

STARMAN: SINS OF THE FATHER
James Robinson/Tony Harris/ Wade von Grawbadger

WONDER WOMAN: THE CONTEST
William Messner-Loebs/Mike Deodato, Jr.

WONDER WOMAN: THE CHALLENGE OF ARTEMIS
William Messner-Loebs/Mike Deodato, Jr.

WONDER WOMAN: SECOND GENESIS
John Byrne

ZERO HOUR: CRISIS IN TIME
Dan Jurgens/Jerry Ordway

OTHER COLLECTIONS OF INTEREST

CAMELOT 3000
Mike W. Barr/Brian Bolland

RONIN
Frank Miller

WATCHMEN
Alan Moore/Dave Gibbons

ARCHIVE EDITIONS

ALL STAR COMICS ARCHIVES VOLUME 1
(ALL STAR COMICS 3-6)
Various writers and artists

ALL STAR COMICS ARCHIVES VOLUME 2
(ALL STAR COMICS 7-10)
Various writers and artists

ALL STAR COMICS ARCHIVES VOLUME 3
(ALL STAR COMICS 11-14)
Various writers and artists

THE FLASH ARCHIVES VOLUME 1
(The Scarlet Speedster's adventures from FLASH COMICS 104, SHOWCASE 4, 8, 13, 14, and THE FLASH 105-108)
John Broome/Robert Kanigher/Carmine Infantino/Frank Giacoia/Joe Giella/Joe Kubert

LEGION OF SUPER-HEROES ARCHIVES VOLUME 1
(The Legion of Super-Heroes' adventures from ADVENTURE COMICS 247, 267, 282, 290, 293, 300-305, ACTION COMICS 267, 276, 287, 289, SUPERBOY 86, 89, 98 and SUPERMAN 147)
Various writers and artists

LEGION OF SUPER-HEROES ARCHIVES VOLUME 2
(The Legion of Super-Heroes' adventures from ADVENTURE COMICS 306-317 and SUPERMAN'S PAL, JIMMY OLSEN 72)
Various writers and artists

LEGION OF SUPER-HEROES ARCHIVES VOLUME 3
(The Legion of Super-Heroes' adventures from ADVENTURE COMICS 318-328, SUPERMAN'S PAL, JIMMY OLSEN 76 and SUPERBOY 117)
Various writers and artists

LEGION OF SUPER-HEROES ARCHIVES VOLUME 4
(The Legion of Super-Heroes' adventures from ADVENTURE COMICS 329-339 and SUPERBOY 124-125)
Various writers and artists

LEGION OF SUPER-HEROES ARCHIVES VOLUME 5
(The Legion of Super-Heroes' adventures from ADVENTURE COMICS 340-349)
Various writers and artists

LEGION OF SUPER-HEROES ARCHIVES VOLUME 6
(The Legion of Super-Heroes' adventures from ADVENTURE COMICS 350-358)
Various writers and artists

LEGION OF SUPER-HEROES ARCHIVES VOLUME 7
(The Legion of Super-Heroes' adventures from ADVENTURE COMICS 359-367 and SUPERMAN'S PAL, JIMMY OLSEN 106)
Various writers and artists